Everything's going to be okay..... Everything is wonderful (Everclear "song" Ozark, 1990ish) .... as long as we're together + you couldn't get rid of me with crabs + gasoline. I love you until the end + we're going to have a fabulous r

D0949630

1254. ...

me

"In *The Win Within*, Dr. Mandelbaum points out the trait that all winners share: a 'don't quit!' attitude, or what he calls the victorious spirit. He shows how everyone can use that focus in their own lives. I've known Bert for years, trusting him both personally and professionally. It's about time he wrote about what it takes to be a winner. Don't quit!"
—**Jake Steinfeld,** chairman of Body by Jake; cofounder of Major League Lacrosse; chairman of the National Foundation for Governors' Fitness Councils

"*The Win Within* shines a light on our inherent need to win, in sports, business, politics, and life. Dr. Mandelbaum's unique view of great athletes' will to win reveals the innate spirit of the human race—a spirit that is cultivated and unleashed in our perennial battle to be the fittest and survive."
—**Reinhold Schmieding,** president and founder of Arthrex

"*The Win Within* is a wonderfully insightful book, written by the brilliant physician and author Bert Mandelbaum. Everyone needs to channel their 'win within'—their will to achieve their dreams as well as overcome life's obstacles and challenges. Dr. Mandelbaum's book shows us how to effectively and triumphantly accomplish these essential goals. *The Win Within* is a must-read for everyone!"
—**Ken Lindner,** author of *Your Killer Emotions: The 7 Steps to Mastering the Toxic Emotions, Urges, and Impulses That Sabotage You*

"*The Win Within* is inspiring, motivational, and just the ticket for psychological renewal! So often we get caught up in defensive living and striving that we lose sight of our true potential for happiness, success, and well-being. This amazing book teaches you that your victorious spirit isn't something you acquire—it's something you release! Fasten your seat belt for an awakening to your true, unrealized potential."
—**Joseph J. Luciani, PhD,** author of *Self-Coaching: The Powerful Program to Beat Anxiety & Depression*

The
WIN
WITHIN

The
WIN
WITHIN

CAPTURING
YOUR
VICTORIOUS
SPIRIT

BERT R. MANDELBAUM, MD

GREENLEAF
BOOK GROUP PRESS

Published by Greenleaf Book Group Press
Austin, Texas
www.gbgpress.com

Distributed by Greenleaf Book Group

For ordering information or special discounts for bulk purchases, please contact Greenleaf Book Group at PO Box 91869, Austin, TX 78709, 512.891.6100.

Design and composition by Greenleaf Book Group
Cover design by Greenleaf Book Group and Debbie Berne
Cover image ©iStockphoto.com/jimkruger

Publisher's Cataloging-In-Publication Data
Mandelbaum, Bert.
    The win within : capturing your victorious spirit / Bert R. Mandelbaum, MD.—First edition.
        pages ; cm
    Issued also as an ebook.
    Includes bibliographical references.
    ISBN: 978-1-62634-131-9
    1. Mandelbaum, Bert.   2. Success—Psychological aspects.   3. Motivation (Psychology)   4. Attitude (Psychology)   5. Athletes—Psychology.   I. Title.

BF637.S8 M36 2014
158.1   2014939303

TreeNeutral®

Part of the Tree Neutral® program, which offsets the number of trees consumed in the production and printing of this book by taking proactive steps, such as planting trees in direct proportion to the number of trees used: www.treeneutral.com

Printed in the United States of America on acid-free paper

14 15 16 17 18 19   10 9 8 7 6 5 4 3 2 1

First Edition

Contents

Acknowledgments

THIS BOOK AND ITS THEME ARE not a compilation of one man's life—they are the culmination of thousands of patients, athletes, coaches, challenges, dilemmas, and games in the sport of life. We learn over and over that life is a journey and that success is always a result of our relationships on and off the field, at the workplace and in the home. After all, life is a team sport! These relationships are the jewels of our lives. My teams have been crucial to my discovery, integration, and success in life.

It starts with my parents, Al and Florence, who I thank for the creation of a loving foundation where our family's values, mission, vision were grounded. My brother, Sam, was my childhood partner growing up in those wonder years, and there was much for us to learn. Thank you to Plainview High's Coaches Wilkens, McNamara, and Goldmeer, who taught me that adversity is the engine of great opportunity and that hard work works.

At SUNY Cortland, led by President Erik Bitterbaum, Barry Batzing, and others, I was inspired to appreciate the biological and marine world and all of its beautiful interactions. The sport of lacrosse has had an important impact on my life through great coaches like Jack Emmer, the late Henry Ciccarone, the late Fred Smith, Joe Townsend, Jerry Schnydman, Mike Riley, Don Zimmerman, and Willie Scroggs.

My gratitude also goes to the Johns Hopkins Bloomberg School of Public Health, for helping me create a path to my career in medicine and sport. To my mentors, Bob Scott, former athletic director and coach at Johns Hopkins, who always mentored me with wisdom and class. To the late Dan Nathans of Johns Hopkins University School of Medicine, a former Nobel laureate who challenged me to refuse to accept anything but the best. To J. Alex Haller, a father of one of my players, Lecky Haller, who showed me the importance of academic translational medicine.

Thank you to the Washington University School of Medicine for teaching me the art, the spirit, and the science of medicine. There, Grant Stevens and Bill Morgan and I became lifelong friends and learned that pleasure and business in life should be one. To the Johns Hopkins Hospital and its orthopaedic surgeons—the late Robby Robinson, the late Lee Riley, Dave Hungerford, Andy Weiland, Vern Tolo, Ken Krackow, and Carl Johnson—who all trained me as a gentleman surgeon with a sense for being a "healer," regardless of the challenge. To my coresidents at Johns Hopkins: Ed Bieber, John Ritterbusch, George White, Mark Myerson, and Bob Hotchkiss—we learned that **T**ogether **E**veryone **A**chieves **M**ore as one **TEAM**. To UCLA's Larry Carter, the late John Wooden, the late Ducky Drake, Tony Spino, and Terry Donahue, who bestowed upon me the philosophy of the Pyramid of Success, on and off the field or court. To those I met during my UCLA fellowship, particularly Jerry Finerman, the late Todd Grant, Jim Puffer, Art Bartolozzi, and Gary Green, who all trained me to become a complete sports doctor.

To all of my present and former fellows who questioned and challenged only to push us to create solutions where there were no answers. To my orthopaedic family and partners at Santa Monica Orthopaedic Group—Ron Gowey, Mike Lain, John Adams, Ken Horacek, John Sellman, Ramin Modabber, Tom Knapp, Kevin Ehrhart, Mike Gerhardt, Arash Lavian, Clint Soppe, and Rachel Triche—with whom I have collaborated and navigated through many of life's challenges, keeping the patient our number-one priority at all times. To my new partners, Neal ElAttrache, Ralph Gambardella, and Steve Shin, and to the Kerlan-Jobe Orthopaedic Clinic partners with whom we have created the new and innovative Institute for Sports Sciences. And to my MD partners, Dave

Schub, Aaron Luber, Stu Holden, and Eric Von Doymi—it is great to create something so special!

To Holly Silvers, Diane Watanabe, Susan Schlegel, Ola Odenjii, Stephanie Insler, and our team at the Santa Monica Sports Foundation, for creating a leadership structure for research, education, and community service. Thanks also to Susan for her creativity and for helping me early on with her energy and editing skills.

To Wayne Wilson, the late John Argue, and Anita DeFrantz of the 1984 Los Angeles Olympics, who supported our first approaches to making it safer for children to play sport.

To Sigi Schmid, who as a UCLA soccer coach got me started with a long and exciting career in the sport of soccer. To Bora Milutinović, Timo Liekoski, Steve Sampson, the late Clive Charles, the late Mooch Myernick, Dave Sarachan, Bob Bradley, Mike Sorber, Pierre Barrieu, and all of the US Soccer coaches whom I have worked with in six men's and two women's World Cups, as well as two Major League Soccer championships. To Bruce Arena: we began as rival high school and college lacrosse players, then became rival college lacrosse coaches before working together with the men's national team in the World Cup and, now, with the LA Galaxy—two sports over forty years and three thousand miles away from our roots. It once again proves that life is a journey and that relationships contribute to success over time.

To all of my medical and sports medicine organizations—including the ICRS, AAOS, AOSSM, AANA, and ISAKOS—for collaboration with countless numbers of colleagues, friends, and peers in leadership, research, innovation, and education.

To US Soccer's Hughie O'Malley, Hank Steinbrecher, Tom King, Dan Flynn, Bill Nuttall, Pam Perkins, Dick Guter, Bob Contiguglia, Burt Haimes, Alan Rothenberg, James Hashimoto, Rudy Rudawsky, Bruce Snell, Dave Andrews, Ivan Pierra, and Sunil Gulati. Together we have shepherded the growth of soccer in the USA since the early 1990s.

To Major League Soccer's Don Garber, Todd Durbin, Mark Abbott, Larry Lemak, and Evan Dabby. We worked tirelessly together to incubate a now very successful professional league.

To FIFA's Sepp Blatter, Jiri Dvorak, Anja Koenig, Monika Muller, and Philipp Tobler, for collaboration and cultivation in our global medical mission of prevention, hope, and wellness.

To Pepperdine University's President Andy Benton, Kevin Wright, and all of the coaches and athletic trainers.

To the United States Olympic Committee, and to Scott Blackmun, Bill Moreau, and Cory Warner, who developed a comprehensive medical and athlete-centric network with me.

To the LA Galaxy and Chivas USA, for working with our medical team, Armando Rivas, Kurt Andrews, and Shunta Shimizu, and our training staff, George Billauer, Eric Pierra, Howard Liebeskind, Tracy Zaslow, Lee Pace, Ray Padilla, Josh Scott, Byron Patterson, Dave Wallis, Sean Kupiec, and William Kim, to improve the health and safety of the players.

To Major League Baseball's Bud Selig, Chris Marinak, John D'Angelo, Gary Green, Keshia Pollack, Frank Curriero, and Jon Coyles, who collaborated with me in establishing programs to answer challenging research issues in today's baseball athletes.

To my team for the 2015 Special Olympics World Games in Los Angeles—Anne Roeser, Jeff Carr, and Pat McClenahan—for their dedication to special-needs athletes. To Maria and Eunice Shriver, who see the athlete in every human being and created the Special Olympics as the venue for this expression.

To former United States presidents Ronald Reagan and Bill Clinton, whose personal interactions inspired me to amplify the importance of consensus building and emotional intelligence in leadership.

To all of the athletes and patients I have worked with, I especially thank you for the collaboration and knowledge of how we discover and integrate the victorious spirit. I am always humbled not by what we have learned but by what we still need to learn for the best care of patients.

To our corporate partners at Johnson & Johnson; DePuy Mitek; DJ Ortho; Arthrex; Smith & Nephew; Össur; Stryker; Exactech; RTI Surgical; AlterG; and Harvest, for your support of our education, research, and community-service programs.

To Reinhold Schmieding, for his dedication to orthopaedic surgeons and improving patient care.

To Johnson & Johnson, for its commitment to and partnership with Safe Kids and the World Cup 2014.

To all of my clinical staff: Susie Pitcher, Marisa Yglesias, Nicole Baggett, Racquel Mabitgang, Monica Modabber, Siobhan Palmer, Anna Rose, and Heather Adle. You are critical to successful patient care.

To Trish Fowler and my entire surgical team at Surgical Center of the Pacific. You work tirelessly with me, case after case, demanding excellence of yourselves and everyone around you. You work and truly live as a team!

To our executive and management team, led by Jeremy Hogue, Rudy Grimaldo, Jay McKim, Rob Obispo, Monica Modabber, and Siobhan Palmer for your collaborative, transformative mission, vision, and core operational plan.

To Providence Saint John's Health Center's Mike Wall, Donna Tuttle, Bob Klein, and all the staff, for creating an outstanding caring environment for all our patients and me.

To Tom Priselac, Rick Jacobs, Bruce Gewertz, Tom Gordon, and their teams at the Cedars-Sinai Health System, for our present and future collaboration.

To agents Frank Breeden and Jan Miller, who have directed and mentored me in this book.

To Paige Stover, for all her help.

To Trace Longo and Sarah Woody of Longo Communications, our very professional PR, marketing, and social media team, who have taught me the creative side of platform creation.

To my Greenleaf team, led by Justin Branch, for believing in this project and for the creative professionalism exhibited by his team of Abby Kitten, Scott James, Ashley Jones, Steve Elizalde, and Bryan Carroll. They are efficient, passionate, and so collaborative in everything they do.

A special thanks to Aaron Hierholzer, for his collaborative vision. He is a truly creative editorial professional.

Thank you to Ken Lindner—and his team, including Shari Freis—for helping with the incubation of my vision, the development of the concept, and seeing it through as a close friend and colleague.

For my longtime friends Marianne and Mitch Wolf, for guidance and support universally.

To Patti and Steve Soboroff, for being out there every morning expressing their win within.

To my sister, Reeva Hunter Mandelbaum, a writer and producer herself. She has been instrumental in writing *The Win Within*. She has grilled me, challenged me creatively, and edited my words when she said they needed to be!

That I have great gratitude for my loving and supportive wife is an understatement. Ruth, a family physician herself, has supported and stood by me through all of my eccentric ideas and habits, crazy work hours, and time away from home. She is an incredible mother and role model to all. Thank you for dotting my i's and crossing my t's and for being the glue that keeps it all together.

To Grandma Annie Sorotzkin, my mother-in-law, a Holocaust survivor—and a thriver. She and Grandpa Josh Sorotzkin have been essential to our family, and I could not have done all of this without you.

Most importantly, immense gratitude to my personal team, my children: Rachel, Jordan, and Ava. It doesn't get any better than you. It's you who taught me that the win is truly within. You are my most valuable players in life and, most importantly, my legacy.

Introduction

GROWING UP AS A THREE-SPORT ATHLETE, playing lacrosse in college, and coaching at Johns Hopkins, all I know is sports. Today, as a sports doctor and an orthopedic surgeon, I repair broken bones, torn cartilage, dislocated shoulders—you know, the things that snap, crunch, shatter, and pop.

My professional life has been devoted to the care of, and research and development of innovative strategies for, athletes at all ages and levels of sport—young and old, recreational and professional, Olympic and collegiate. Some I fix so they can return to play in a World Cup and professional sports; some so they can keep up their Sunday hike in the canyons.

After thousands and thousands of cases, I've seen severe injury, immense struggle, dramatic recovery, and the incredible spirit of victory that propels my patients through it all. It's become clear to me that anything can happen to anyone at any time—injury, illness, adversity can sneak up on us without warning, and even when we do expect them. They're often even harder than we anticipated, and yet, I've also seen many people boldly take on the journey through adversity. I've seen elite athletes accomplish almost unthinkable recoveries, and I've seen my non-professional athletes find their own inner victories that are, for them, just as life changing.

People often ask me about the behind-the-scenes mechanics of my work with elite athletes. They want to know the mysterious process that motivates the extraordinary among us. How do they reach such high levels of performance? And how do they go from a devastating injury to return-to-play? How do they stick it out when they suffer a setback that would put others out of the arena for good? The short version is this: They marshal their inner victorious spirit—a resource that is inside all of us—to push through setbacks and perform at peak levels, physically and mentally. They capitalize on the genetic legacy of survival and perseverance that's part of our collective history, using their biological drive not just to survive, but also to thrive. They recognize that being a victor is most about the taking part in the sport of life, about enjoying the journey, the highs and the lows, without worrying about the destination.

For years, I'd been quietly observing these principles in action through my work as a sports physician, but it wasn't until I got an out-of-the-blue request that I started thinking about how to coherently express what the "victorious spirit" is and how we can nurture it in ourselves. It was a typical Tuesday afternoon in January just a few years ago, when my cell phone rang. It was a busy day at the clinic, as usual, but I had a moment between patients, so I answered.

"Hello," said the voice on the other end of the line, "this is Erik Bitterbaum, the president of the State University of New York at Cortland." He then asked whether I was sitting down. A sinking feeling came over me. I felt like a nightmare was unfolding. I walked into the next room and immediately sat down, bracing myself for bad news. What had happened? What was the problem? My heart raced as I listened intently to his words: "Congratulations, Dr. Mandelbaum. You've been selected to receive an Honorary Doctorate of Humane Letters and give a graduation speech in May."

I took a long breath, sighing with gratitude. In that one micromoment, my plethora of negative emotions had been transformed into a wave of relief and gratefulness at the honor the university saw fit to give me. I hastily thanked him and told him I'd be happy to give the graduation speech. As the phone call ended with a smile, I slowly placed the phone on my desk, gazed out the window, and realized that I already knew what my address would be about: the spirit of victory I saw in the athletes I worked with, and how the same spirit can enrich the life of anyone.

Standing before that crowd of young, optimistic faces, I laid out my ideas: how we're all bred for success, how we all have an inner athlete, and how there are actions we can take to strengthen our victorious spirit. These themes apparently resonated with the graduates, the parents, and faculty—the energy was palpable, with each phase ending in a thunderous applause. That speech, and the reaction to it, sparked the urge in me to flesh out these concepts fully—into the book you now hold in your hands.

My intent within these pages is to show you what I've observed, in the trenches and in the training room, about the victorious spirit that drives elite athletes to attain physical and mental greatness. I want to show you that the tools they use aren't mysterious and that their practices are doable by everybody. You'll read about how David Beckham rapidly recovered from a torn Achilles tendon prior to back-to-back LA Galaxy championships. You will see how the underdog US Men's Soccer Team used optimism as a tool in the run-up to Landon Donovan's ninety-first minute goal to get to the second round of the 2010 World Cup in South Africa. You'll witness the inspiring journeys of Olympic athletes Tim Daggett and Cliff Meidl, both of whom refused to give up when devastating physical setbacks threatened to take them out of the sports they loved.

You might be thinking, "Well, I'm not David Beckham or Tim Daggett." Of course you're not. Neither am I. They're inimitable. But, we all have much to learn from their stories, even if you have no professional athletic goals of any sort. Experience has taught me that we're all athletes—even the most ordinary among us—and that we're all navigating through the life of sports and the sport of life, connected to ancient imprints hardwired in us a long time ago. We run all kinds of races, literally and metaphorically. Sometimes at full sprint, sometimes sluggish, and every now and then, limping. We each engage in a personal journey of success, defeat, recovery, and growth, where purpose is more about the process than the result.

Many of you are faced with financial burdens, professional setbacks, health issues, family problems, and a variety of other diverse challenges that often arrive unexpectedly. These problems, sometimes shocking in nature, can in many ways put an end to your plans and goals, and cause you to lose your will and your focus on survival. How does a person react when they are diagnosed with cancer? How does a person find the will to run when they have lost both their legs? Where does a person find the confidence to compete in Olympic-level competitions against athletes half their age? These types of questions were asked of many of the individuals in this book, and we'll see how they answered: in short, they found the "win within."

The principles in this book apply holistically to your life, because that win within—your victorious spirit—has less to do with your physical body and much more to do with what's inside, including those unmistakable genes. So no matter your size, health status, age, gender, or interest in organized sports, you can use the tools of elite athletes to discover and enhance your own inner victor.

One of my patients, an award-winning television producer with several hit shows, struggled with weight issues from childhood. It impacted her health, joints, and gait. I fixed an orthopedic problem, and set a course for rehab. I also took the opportunity to talk to her about overall well-being. I mentioned that she might not know it, but she's intrinsically hardwired to be an athlete. I told her that she'd already mastered how to channel the forces of will and determination, as seen in other parts of her life, and that it's a matter of adapting what she already has to this kind of project: herself! She started with small accomplishments, walks and hikes, and in time progressed to running. Now, she's fallen in love with it, never having believed that she could be a fifty-plus woman, jogging up and down hills, showing up as her best self.

My patient learned what I learned and what you can learn: The most common triage responses elite athletes employ to get back on track soon after injury are not mysterious and do not involve superpowers.

They're simple, commonsense responses to reset focus, problem solve, and face challenges.

I know these principles work because I've seen them in play firsthand—not just in my patients but also in myself.

• • •

Snowbird, Utah. It's been a great day of skiing. When I'm done, I stop to watch my youngest daughter, Ava, on the bunny hill. I'm watching her laughing and I'm so happy and focused that I don't see the out-of-control snowboarder racing in my direction. Whack! I'm struck from the side, just in my blind spot. I fly forward and land with a terrible thud on the cold snow.

I'm motionless. A burning, numbing sensation radiates down my left side. In the minutes it takes for patrol to get to me, I slip into default surgeon-mode. "So this is what an L5 disc injury feels like," I think. I can already tell that my disc has gone out—*avulsed* is the medical term—and is obstructing my nerve root. I'm in shock, but I'm also cognizant of three other very important things:

1. I'm not okay.

2. I can't get up and I can't walk.

3. Surgery is inevitable.

Mostly, I'm aware that in a split second my life as I know it has changed. I'm just praying the damage isn't irreparable. For a lifelong jock like myself, someone who relies on his daily run for energy and inspiration, this would be devastating.

Once my family finds me and sees that I'm badly injured, I'm taken straight to the hospital. One week later, I have surgery on my back, and in two more days I'm released from the hospital and home recovering. The operation went well—or as well as could be expected. I'm still going to be out of commission for quite some time. One morning shortly after my release, I'm sprawled out on the chaise in the backyard, the dogs at my feet. My wife is at work, the kids at school. I'm forced to rest—not my strong suit. I'm in a funk. Impatient.

The irony is not lost on me. I have been on the other side, thousands of times. The cheerleader. The holder of the vision. The in-charge, you-can-do-it, and this-is-how doctor. I admit it: I'm not liking the view from this side. I'm not liking this total loss of control. At all.

Later that day, my surgeon—who's also a friend—calls with updates. I ask him the same question I'm asked routinely: "When can I run again?"

Silence.

"You can't."

It wasn't "You can't for now." It wasn't "You can't, but . . . ." It was just "You can't." Period.

My daily run is critical to everything I do. I live a somewhat Spartan life. My work requires long hours on my feet, a fast pace, and the job is physically demanding. Running is intrinsic to my resilience, fortitude, and emotional balance. But mostly, I'm like all runners and weekend jocks—it's my thing. I look forward to it. It's the endorphins, the rush, my *Rocky* moment when I reach the top of the neighborhood hill and stretch my arms to the sky.

You can't.

My *Rocky* moment starts unwinding before my eyes. In slow motion, step by step, backwards. Down, down, down all the summits I'd achieved, down the steps of my life, down my mountain, until it's just me at the bottom, staring at the impossible climb.

It's not just the disappointment that I can't run anymore, but I'm a type-A guy, the hard-charger archetype. My mandate is "I can!" I push myself to the limits, too much, even. I'm not ready for this—not me, not yet. It doesn't even feel like me. Deep down, I know the only constant is change, but this change is tough to swallow.

You would think that with all I've seen and all I know, this would be easy.

No. It's not. In fact, it's horrible. I know intellectually what it takes to recover from something like this—I've seen elite athletes do it many times. But I can't find a way to connect that to my current reality. I'm pissed. My spirit is shut down. My confidence is wrecked.

This much I know—I need to get moving, regardless of how crappy I feel on all levels. I know that's the first step, and I make it, after great effort. I struggle to the door and pick up the cane. I limp carefully and very slowly down the small steps. The dogs are wagging their tails and run out ahead of me.

And?

Well, like most life-altering epiphanies, mine happens unexpectedly.

At first, I limp very slowly, up the block and back, on a flat surface. I'm a little bit impressed with myself because I know I'm walking pretty well, considering the level of injury and the usual timeline of recovery. I have to laugh that I'm surprised. This is rehab boot camp. I know this. I tell my patients all the time the importance of developing daily exercise habits in the best of times, as they'll serve you well in the worst of times. It's true and I'm elated. Just being able to do that short walk, even with the expectations adjusted for where I am, is an accomplishment. One doable goal set and met. I'm inspired. I'm progressing.

My spirit gets back in the game. My momentum is recharged. I have that magic that I see in athletes as they perform at the top of their game and overcome their physical challenges: the victorious spirit.

Over the course of the next few weeks, I add more goals and accomplishments—longer walks, then hikes, and swimming. I finally feel ready to get on my bike and I do—and I'm great for a long time.

Then one day, I'm again reminded of what I mentioned earlier—that anything can happen at any time. I'm happily tooling down the surface streets in town on my bike, when out of nowhere a car hits me. The driver didn't see me; I didn't see him. Once I get back up and assess the damage, I see that I was banged and bruised, requiring rest, but that nothing was broken or reinjured. Yet it rattles my confidence. A month earlier I'd never been hit, and now suddenly it's like I'm a moving target. There I am, back on the chaise, with the dogs at my feet. I'm feeling beyond vulnerable. Like I've lost my mojo. Or worse—like I've lost my sense of who I am.

But after a couple of days of rest, my spirit resurfaces. I'm reminded of what I tell my patients: "Stay the course, and when an obstacle comes up, respond with 'What now?' rather than 'What if?' Restrategize and readjust." A few days later I'm ready to reverse the backslide. I turn this way, I'm okay, turn that way, I'm okay. How do I feel? I feel good. Am I confident? Check. It's my own calculated leap of faith and I return to action. I go out to the garage, strap on the helmet, snap on the back brace, and force myself back into battle and onto the bike.

Our town is known for the 5- and 10-K races it holds every Fourth of July. That summer after the injury, when my wife and kids were putting on their running shoes, and out the door by 7:00 a.m., I was suiting up with them. But instead of running, I reset my head to another goal, bypassing the temptation to focus on what I couldn't participate in, and instead strapping on my helmet and riding to the top of the mountain.

· · ·

There is nothing to prevent you from attaining feelings of greatness, mastering the awe of your peers, or shivering with pleasure from the mighty sensation of good health. All this comes when you uncover your inner athlete and capture the victorious spirit that's already inside you. Every one of us can be a victor, no matter what position we're starting from or where we end up. All it takes is struggle and forward movement—a refusal to give in to inertia and despair.

I return frequently to the words of Pierre de Coubertin, founder of the modern Olympics: "The important thing is not to win, but to take part. The important thing in life is not triumph, but the struggle. The essential thing is not to have conquered, but to have fought well."

In Part I of this book, we'll look at how we can each discover the victorious spirit inside ourselves. Whether you think so or not, it's there—fostered by eons of evolutionary history. We'll see that injury and illness are actually like a forge that burns within each of us—something we can use to make us magnificent and strong. We'll see that the win within can bind us together to give rise to an even greater victorious spirit.

Then, in Part II, we'll delve into what I call the "Big Five": the five areas of life that super-performers focus on to access their win within. You'll see that when you tend to each of these domains of life and use the tactics that elite athletes do, you'll be able to tap into the same power, and use it to thrive in every area of life.

Finally, in Part III, I'll give you a process to start directly integrating the Big Five into your daily life. This is the "Mission, Vision, Plan" or "MVP" process, and it will help you keep your victorious spirit alive and growing as you become your own most valuable player.

The best part of all of this is that there's nothing to buy, nothing to obtain, no further equipment to acquire, and no complicated process to learn. You just have to discover and nurture the victorious spirit for yourself—to find your win within.

PART I

SUMMONING THE VICTORIOUS SPIRIT

CHAPTER 1

Hardwired for Victory
A Genetic Legacy of Athleticism

BOSTON, MASSACHUSETTS, APRIL 2001. I'M THE doctor at the Boston Marathon finish line. Just behind me, hundreds of doctors and nurses are ready to respond with me to falling or fallen athletes. It's two hours past the starting gun, and I'm swept up in the anticipation and deafening cheers of the thousands of supporters, spectators, families, friends, and colleagues. Lee Bong-Ju of South Korea clocks in at 2:09:43, and a few minutes later, Catherine Ndereba of Kenya clocks in at 2:23:53. For hours, with each subsequent runner, the noise-level builds wildly— a celebration of each achievement. While there's only one winner, each of the fifteen thousand runners are victors to me. Simply by participating, by engaging in the struggle, every one of these runners has found their win within.

Standing outside the medical tent, I'm experiencing a sense of my own journey. The Boston Marathon is an iconic race, and it's an honor for me to be selected as the finish-line physician. It's particularly significant because Boston is the home of my personal hero: Dr. Paul Dudley White, the father of American preventative cardiology, who in 1924 was one of the founders of the American Heart Association and the maverick pioneer of the personal fitness concept. (Believe it or not, in the time of Dr. White, exercise for well-being was still a new thing!)

The glory of this and every marathon is far less about the finish line, than it is the 26.2 miles that precede it: the preparation, the anticipation, the start, the run, the crowd, the supporters, the challenge, the triumph, and the memory. Each runner approaches the finish line exhausted, legs wobbly and cramped, but with a surge of endorphins and confidence. The monumental reality of the extraordinary achievement of finishing the race overtakes the pain.

But what is the origin of this exuberance—in both the runners and the spectators? Why are so many driven to sign up for the race, to push themselves to some unknown parameter of ability? Why spend all that time training, all that pain going beyond their previous ability level? And why are the throngs of people watching so hyped up? They're not the ones running, so what's with the enthusiasm?

The answer to all these questions lies in the fact that we're all born to be athletes, and it's hardwired in our genes, woven into a complicated twisting of our DNA with those double helixes and molecules. You might make deeply personal choices about exercise and fitness, but participation in sport—actively or even as a spectator—connects us to who we intrinsically are, biologically, chemically, spiritually, and socially.

The type of physical activity you choose doesn't matter. You might be, like me, one of the half million finishers at the almost three hundred marathons across America—from the Moose's Tooth in Alaska, to a dark highway in the cooled down Nevada desert, at ET Full Moon Midnight Marathon. Or you might compete in an obstacle course, triathlon, or relay. Or maybe you're one of the over five million Americans to compete in fun and mud runs. Maybe you just enjoy hiking up the hill at the end of your block. Whatever the case, these activities give you a chance to access a win within, access the part of you that's hardwired genetically and anatomically like the most elite athletes. That access is how we thrive.

I've been in the stands at the Olympics, the World Cup, and championship games, and while there, I've thought a lot about what happens when we watch elite runners, gymnasts, swimmers, or football players run that fast, jump that high, or show that kind of strength and grace. Invariably, we're amazed and awed. Something in us is moved at a very deep level. We're inspired. We want to *be like them*. We find that our bodies connect us in that moment. Indeed, we converse, think, and wonder, but it is the physical manifestations—the bodies, the smiles, the laughter, the winks, the curves, and the muscles—that hit us with the most force. The body might be the most wonderful thing on earth, especially when it comes to linking us together with our common past.

The reason that this urge, this spirit, wells up within us is because it's familiar—in the truest sense of the word: the athlete we're watching is an ancient family member who shares our DNA and its network of potentialities. This mysterious drive weaves its way into our consciousness, because at our core, we are all athletes.

Athletes inspire across the human spectrum because it is the athletes who possess that innate image of success, and it is they who symbolize the greatness that our bodies possess. From birth, we are blessed with one of nature's masterpieces: the human body. When we see Michael Phelps swim to Olympic victory, time and time again, we relate. We are both human. When we see Usain Bolt launch himself across the finish line at blazing speed, we relate. We are both human. And if one human can achieve such greatness, our mind tells us, we—also being human— have a chance at it too. All of us, at some point, have been driven by such dreams, beginning with the pilots, astronauts, scientists, and athletes we admired in childhood.

We are hardwired to survive and, consequently, to compete. Something magical happens to those of us who do not have extraordinary gifts when we watch those who do. We connect at a visceral level to that victorious spirit that resides in the heart of everyone.

So what is it that separates us from Olympic gold? It is none other than an ability to unlock the victorious spirit within. You embody this legacy—an ancient, invisible wiring—as does the marathon runner, launching him- or herself across the finish line. The part of you that was a hunter, for whom exercise was an essential part of survival, is in you.

ATHLETICISM ONCE EQUALED SURVIVAL:
THE KHOISAN OF THE KALAHARI

Early in the history of our species, we developed an integrated response to the natural threats of the wild. We stood. We pursued. We ran. We fought to attain sustenance and survival in an unforgiving environment.

Africa is the setting for the long dawn of human history and our Darwinian evolutionary sequence. Four million years ago, apelike creatures named *Australopithecus* walked upright on that continent. They were an intermediate species, between apes and humans. Two million years ago, the first creatures to be classified as part of the human species—*Homo erectus*—evolved in Africa. They developed a technology based on sharp tools of flint, introducing what has become known as the Stone Age. The Lower Paleolithic era took place somewhere around one hundred thousand years ago, as *Homo sapiens*—how we are classified—replaced *Homo erectus*. This final step in the evolutionary process occurred just after the Khoisan people appeared in Southern Africa, in and around the Kalahari Desert. This group, which demonstrates the largest genetic diversity of all human populations, is now recognized as one of the first lineages to branch from the main human family tree, developing in relative isolation and preserving the lineage of millennia prior. And because they live today much like they did thousands of years ago, they give us a fascinating glimpse into our past.[1]

Today, every human, Khoisan or not, remains very close in makeup to our ancient ancestors, no matter how differently we're living! Genetically, modern-day humans are almost identical to these pre-agricultural hunter-gatherers, who thrived in their environment. These early human families roamed the plains and savannahs in clans, focused on survival, and, as some believe, their quality of life.

Thirty thousand years ago, there was a seemingly endless supply of animal life and edible plants as the early human families migrated with the game herds and hunted what they needed to survive. When they weren't hunting, they watched the stars, told stories around the fire, and painted their dreams on the walls of caves. High levels of intelligence were required to make tools and find prey.

For their part, the Khoisan had a formidable reputation as pursuit hunters and trackers. They could follow the spoor—the tracks or scent—of an animal across virtually any kind of surface or terrain. Their extraordinary skills enabled them to distinguish between the spoor of a wounded animal and that of the rest of the herd. Khoisan hunters also needed to be endurance runners in extreme conditions of heat and drought. They had to successfully adapt to the challenges of hydration, selective electrolyte and nutritional requirements, and the bodily response to fatigue, heat, and cold. Their bodies had to be multilevel performance machines with mental, physical, and emotional stamina in order to be successful. If one of the Khoisan was injured or determined not fit, they were left behind and became something else's dinner.

Let's take a closer look at one member of this early human group. We find our Khoisan hunter in the Kalahari Desert in pursuit of an impala. It's three hours into the hunt and he is tired, hot, and dehydrated. But thanks to his fine-tuned levels of fitness from years of strenuous activity, endorphins are released in his brain. Instantaneously, he surges into another gear, charging up the hill as his mood elevates. Just like the marathon runners approaching the finish line, he knows he can do it. On the top of the hill, the impala, an animal adapted for sprints and short bursts of energy, has started to weaken from the relentless pursuit of the hunter. Overheated, fatigued, and trapped, the impala finally succumbs to the Khoisan hunter's spear and becomes his prey. The fallen animal provides sustenance to this highly evolved human competitor.

Our hunter must now get his kill—and himself—back to camp. Fortunately, he's learned that he can rehydrate by drinking the salt-rich blood of the impala, essential sustenance to stabilize his depleted system. Once again it is the hunter over the hunted; one of many innate physiological adaptations in our modern brains designed to keep us alive.

In *Nature* magazine, in 2004, evolutionary biologists Daniel Lieberman and Dennis Bramble explored the expressed physical traits that make us "born to run," and really good at this kind of impala-chasing endurance.[2] Our early human ancestors used endurance to chase prey to exhaustion. This worked for scavenging too. Their premise is that in the savannah ancestors would compete with hyenas—also good long-distance runners—to get to an animal carcass. The theory tells the story behind our springy Achilles tendons, hairlessness, and ability to sweat. Semicircular canals in the inner ear also help us balance as we run. Our modern adaptations of ancient wirings are still at work. Experiments that measure the activity of the gluteus maximus muscles in volunteers during a walk and a jog find that walking does almost nothing, but when running, the glutes fire up. We've also seen—astonishingly—that the brain fires up with more activity when operating the glutes than with any other lower-extremity muscles.

All these findings confirm what we have observed and have been talking about for years. As Lieberman and Bramble write: "Running has deep evolutionary roots. Although humans no longer need to run, the capacity and proclivity to run marathons is the modern manifestation of a uniquely human trait that help make humans the way we are."[3]

The good thing is that evolution took into account that humans need a little extra motivation across the hot desert. You have probably at some point in your life experienced what's widely described as "runners' high" or a flow of endorphins during aerobic exercise. This is because those activities produce "endocannabinoids"—narcotic-like pleasure chemicals. In the *Journal of Experimental Biology*, David Raichlen from the University of Arizona suggests that those chemicals are intrinsic to the evolution of the brain, and may have helped make humans turn into long-distance runners. He states: "Our evolutionary history appears to have included this kind of endurance activity and rewarded it. And as a result, we continue to have a biological imperative (to move)."[4] Exertion kicked in our brain's reward centers, so not only are we hardwired with the anatomy to be active, we're hardwired to enjoy it!

You might not be in shape, but you have the genetic stuff and potential to be a long-distance runner, or at least an around-the-block jogger, or a hiker or biker, a yogalini or a skateboarder. Lieberman suggests that our love of sports is partly an outgrowth of our running past. "Animals play at things that are important to them," he says, "and we play at running."[5]

In the biological journey of our lives, we're programmed to thrive. And it's always there—inside of you—a switch you can turn on at any time, at any place or level, and in the face of any challenge. From the time you're born, a miraculous sequence of progressive, purposeful, structural, and functional events develop your systems—brain, nervous, circulatory, hormonal, and musculoskeletal. The miracle of these synchronized events, along with a dynamic balance of emotional, spiritual, and psychological integrity, is what we describe as health.

This isn't to say that the win within is just about doing physical activity. The victorious spirit encompasses our whole being—our physical bodies, mental proclivities, our internal drives and spiritual directives. The point is that we should all feel ownership of the history of our species and understand that the very specific genetic makeup that helped our ancestors succeed is still very much present in us. When we start regarding ourselves as born athletes and natural survivors, we're in a better position to overcome the challenges of life and reach our peaks.

WHAT DOES SURVIVAL MEAN TODAY?

As a sports doctor and orthopedic surgeon who understands the human body on the mechanical and evolutionary level, I've always held the opinion that we're born to be athletes. Research in genetics is now illuminating why—the Human Genome Project, for example, completed in 2003, mapped thousands of regions of DNA, identifying the biological foundations for where our athletic abilities—like speed, strength, and endurance—reside. But there's still the human factor—the personal challenge for each of us in how to leverage this information, and the practical application in daily life. How can I help my patient—from the professional soccer player who is injured, to the seventy-five-year-old hiker—use his or her intrinsic gifts to summon the win within?

Today, of course, we no longer have to hunt for food and migrate with our food supply. We find that we were designed as a species for physical high-performance activity and, yet, we are now living in an environment in which the opportunities to be physically active are diminishing. We are also faced with challenges that can cause our spirits to wane and our dreams to become clouded and misguided.

As we formed societies, tribes, and cities and towns, our physical development became less of an imperative for survival. We formed social contracts, developed infrastructures, and created technologies. Our abilities to outrun predators and catch prey took on new expressions once we transcended, as Abraham Maslow called it, the "hierarchy of basic needs" like shelter and food. Despite progress, our inherent drives—instilled within us for thousands of generations—have remained active. Athletic experiences and sports are the outlets for our shared biological drive. We now develop our athleticism through brains and emotions, as well as power and endurance.

In the true Darwinian laws of adaptation, the only constant in life is change. Generation after generation, life brings new issues of social, physical, and economic challenges: famine, war, upheaval, disease, and apathy, the maladies of our modern world. With our march out of the bush and into the suburban and urban jungle, our minds and bodies are evolving, albeit slowly. Today, success in our society is not measured in the kill, but in the self-proclaimed win. It is not about the win itself, but about the victory, and once we discover that, we learn that the win is truly about the victorious spirit: a multilevel, comprehensive, all-inclusive mind and body experience.

As such, we, as individuals and as a species, are hardwired to be survivors. This is how the life of sport and the sport of life are inextricably linked. The fact that our human spirit can succeed over the toughest challenges is part of our heritage.

CHAPTER 2

Mend It Like Beckham

Using the Victorious Spirit
to Come Back from Adversity

IT'S FALL, 1987. I'M WAITING AT the UCLA hospital. The operating room is prepped. The patient I'm waiting for is Tim Daggett, the Olympic gold medal gymnast, returning from a devastating fall. His plane should've landed at LAX by now, after an eleven-hour direct flight from Rotterdam where he'd been competing. Instead, it's been circling Los Angeles for an hour in extreme turbulence caused by rainstorms. Just when I think it can't get worse, it gets a lot worse. The plane can't land; it's being detoured to Las Vegas. We quickly mobilize an ambulance to transport him six hours across the desert.

You might know Tim Daggett as a sports commentator. I met him when he was a UCLA student and competing in the 1984 Summer Olympics in Los Angeles. He clinched the US Men's Gymnastics Team's gold medal with his flawless high bar routine, completed with a perfectly stuck landing. The victory remains an indelible moment in Tim's career and in Olympic history. In 1987, Tim was twenty-five, and a critical member of the US Men's Gymnastics Team. Then, in Rotterdam, he attempted a piked Cuervo vault, a handspring into a half-twist and backflip. He launched himself into the air but landed slightly off balance and snapped his leg in two. After two difficult surgeries in Europe, he was coming back home for the last. Finally, the ambulance arrived from Las Vegas, and we found Tim in a very bad state. We operated for the third time and reset his leg. The next days were the skin grafts.

Just two weeks later, his spirit marshaled and he was on the way to healing: Tim was ready to go home. It was amazing. My awe was captured by a reporter in a *Los Angeles Times* article about Tim's accident. This is an excerpt of what I said:

> Tim is the quintessence of the individual who attacks an insurmountable goal. For him it is almost symbolic. The symbol is a man conquering his environment. Give him a challenge, and Tim will conquer it . . . There is something intrinsic to a world-class gymnast. They have a unique ability to identify a goal, create a plan and execute that plan. That's why Tim is successful. Adversity, no problem. A ruptured disk, no problem. A broken leg, no problem. He has a very positive attitude.

In rereading my words, I'm struck by the fact that I'd started to formulate the idea that provides the foundation for this book and that Tim exemplifies: triumphing over injury, staying on course, and following a dream is a journey with steps to be mastered. Tim—voted into the Olympic Hall of Fame in 2005—inspired me then and inspires me now. Bearing witness to his recovery was a painful, formative, and humbling experience for me as a young sports doctor.

You can read the details in Tim's great memoir, *Dare to Dream/ Tragedy and Triumph*, but by the time of his Rotterdam accident, Tim had already faced his share of physical problems, including ankle repairs and a dangerously ruptured disk in his neck. Most other athletes would've retired from competition after the Olympic gold. He'd already heard this suggestion from his doctors, mother, and friends. Yet he consistently responded with a dogged refusal.

But the Rotterdam incident threatened to decisively finalize his career. The broken bone severed an artery and pierced through his skin, a severe compound fracture. I went to work putting his bones back together. While I knew that he would walk again, elite-level competition seemed unlikely.

Filled with an angry defiance, Tim met the challenge of each phase of his rehabilitation, unwilling to settle for anything less than a full recovery and a return to competition. His tenacity, at first received doubtfully by our team of physicians, eventually convinced us that his desire to return to gymnastics was much more than mere fantasy. Tim was determined. He proved himself worthy of the nickname his UCLA teammates had given him: the Raging Bull. Whatever the obstacle—an open fracture, vascular injury, compartment syndrome—Tim stood unshaken.

I told him that we would treat him like an athlete, not as a patient, with the goal to get him to Seoul for the 1988 Summer Olympics. It was a grounded realism. Even if no one could predict what would happen or whether or not he could do it, I thought he could. My optimism was a tool and motivator.

Typically, compound fractures require a minimum recovery period of a full year. By the end of seven months, Tim not only walked flawlessly but was back in the gym training vigorously to make the Olympic Games. Surpassing this already astounding feat of dedication, he reached the Olympic trials in Salt Lake City. His team, including me, joined and supported him through every routine. I was breathless and fearful as he performed almost faultlessly, but he came up just shy, missing qualification by one point.

Tim was still a victor. He reached the trials and he kept moving forward. He embodied the spirit that confronts adversity head on. He remained fully cognizant of the potential for disappointment but harnessed that potential as a force of motivation rather than despondency. He willingly opted to seek out an uncertain triumph over a secure mediocrity. Tim, like the title of his book, dared to dream.

He commanded his journey, decided his own dreams, wrote his own ending, and left his Olympic adventure on his own terms: walking away having made a heroic effort, not on a stretcher.

THE ENGINE OF THE SPIRIT:
A TOOL FOR RECOVERY

In the previous chapter, we saw that the victorious spirit is our evolutionary birthright, an inner strength inherent to our nature as human beings. But sometimes forces like age, accidents, and misfortune can weaken our spirit and hold us back. Everyone has experienced loss and disappointment at some point in their life. Sometimes we fall short when reaching for our goals, due to bad luck or an obstacle that was impossible to anticipate. These types of adversity are often the biggest barriers to achieving our goals. In these situations, we have to hold on tight and ensure that our spirit never falters, and that our dreams stay fresh, alive, and burning, much like Tim Daggett's did.

The incredible, and perhaps counterintuitive, thing about the victorious spirit is that it can actually be fueled by adversity rather than crushed by it. If you remember the physical and mental strength you possess as a member of the human race, you can turn your adversity into opportunity and succeed at life like an elite athlete succeeds in sport.

Don't take the easy way out by making excuses and giving up. No one invites adversity into their lives, and while you can't always be as prepared for it as you would like to be, the victorious spirit enables you to turn this bad luck into opportunity. Adversity is never the end, but rather a catalyst for you to push yourself further than you may have even thought possible. You simply need to unlock the victorious spirit.

Throughout my career, I've worked with athletes of all shapes and sizes. These individuals live in a world of high stakes, hard play, competition, and top performance. Everything's intensified. Their jobs require amped-up feats of will, energy, and determination, forces of the human spirit that are intrinsic to being victorious in all circumstances, on the field or off. When seemingly invincible athletes get unlucky, sports doctors see them at their most vulnerable, and we also see how they come back from the blow. Whether it's an injury on the field, a game-changing fall, or a bad moment with irrevocable consequences, the journey—like all journeys—is tough, full of obstacles, and unpredictable. Always. Even for the fittest of the fit.

This journey requires the engine of the spirit as much as it requires weight lifting, treadmills, and ice baths. But what is the spirit? People far more adept than I am in these matters have pondered the question— philosophers, spiritual and religious leaders. I don't know what it is, but I view the spirit as a tool that drives us forward, toward our goals and dreams. From a surgeon's perspective, medicine is about technical mechanics and science. But it's also about art, intuition, the human heart, and miracles. To me, working with great athletes—especially when they're facing a huge setback—is about human transcendence, improbable dreams, and supporting sometimes unreasonable journeys with reasonable courses of action. It's always a calculated leap of faith, but the important thing is to take it.

The steps of the journey from any injury are fundamentally the same, whether it's your ten-year-old or an NFL quarterback, an Olympian or a middle school soccer player—each follows the same path, despite any incidental differences of specific activity, age, ability, race, or culture: they dare to dream, they rally their spirit, and they keep progressing toward their goals and participating in the sport of life— no matter what.

DAVID BECKHAM AND THE POWER OF PROGRESSION

When a professional athlete is injured, whether it's a star like Tim Daggett or any player on the roster of any team, there are a lot of details, dilemmas, conflicts, and challenges. I'm part of the team's team—a mix of physicians, trainers, physical therapists, nutritionists, chiropractors, podiatrists, dentists, sports psychologists, and exercise physiologists— which is tasked with navigating these complex issues. Together with the injured athlete, we approach rehabilitation holistically and comprehensively, building synergy between our respective disciplines. We ask the player, "How do you feel? How's your confidence?" Then we look at MRIs and test for range of motion, strength, stamina, side-to-side movement, soreness, and ability to run, jump, and hop. One of the most important things we do together is establish a set of interconnected goals designed to keep the athlete progressing until their performance reaches the desired level.

Recovery from an injury follows a template similar to that of daily performance enhancement. We are always progressively creating and meeting new goals and guideposts, elevating physical standards with respect to stamina, strength, and jumping ability by testing the athlete and identifying and correcting weaknesses. This doesn't just involve physical practices but also psychological ones, including visualization and other techniques. For example, an athlete might not play for three months, but he might nevertheless be visualizing—envisioning himself playing on the field—during each practice and game.

This process of forward progression, meeting small goals along the way to our big goal, was coded and recoded in us as we participated in a Darwinian race to survive. Evolution designed us to realize and optimize our intrinsic potential—to experience, improve, surpass, and create new limits of performance. This concept of progressive advancement is used in training rooms all the time with professional athletes because it's organic. We prepare for games and upcoming challenges one quantum more difficult than we will play, and we train by gradually elevating specific standards. This is how most of us progress and thrive in life, as this is not a matrix reserved just for elite athletes. Any of us can find our inner athlete and use this approach to come back, step by step, from any kind of adversity. We can all dare to set a big, scary goal and then work out a series of steps to get us there. It's the victorious spirit that drives this process and that's an integral part of finding the win within. I'll always remember one of the most dramatic times I saw this process at work: in superstar athlete David Beckham.

It's the 2011 championship game for professional soccer team the LA Galaxy. I'm on the sidelines, watchful and concerned as #23, Beckham, sprints across the slippery field. Like always during competition, my first-responder instincts are fully engaged—a "hope for the best, prepare for the worst" mindset until each player gets through the clock uninjured.

In Beckham's case, there are specific stakes and vulnerabilities. The previous year he ruptured his Achilles and made an amazing comeback. But as a surgeon I know that each post-injury return presents a new vulnerability. Even when all the boxes are checked, tests passed, and confidences restored. The numbers for Beckham are clear: this is a devastating injury and each game presents an approximate 15 percent chance at re-injury; any return-to-play is a calculated leap of faith, not a guarantee. I'm hoping it holds.

The injury happened when David Beckham was loaned to professional Italian soccer club A.C. Milan during an LA Galaxy hiatus—a common practice in professional soccer during off-seasons. In 2010, A.C. Milan was ahead 1–0 against their Italian rivals Chievo Verona, and with only ten minutes to go, David Beckham went down. I was watching the game on television and saw the agony on Beckham's face—it was obvious that something was seriously wrong. When he reached the sideline, he crumpled to the ground. I watched as officials examined his left leg and carried him off on a stretcher. I didn't know exactly what had happened, but I knew it was a game changer.

I soon learned he'd completely ruptured his left Achilles tendon. The traditional treatment of that injury, after surgery and a period of rest, is physical therapy for about a year before returning to the field. Beckham had a long road ahead of him.

Before coming back to Los Angeles, Beckham traveled to Turku, Finland, for surgery performed by Dr. Sakari Orava. It was successful, and he walked out of the hospital in a cast with the aid of crutches. When he returned to rehab with us in Los Angeles, he was motivated and focused, attacking goals with his own set of expectations.

One of the things I've observed is that the trademark of a triumphant spirit is that it declares itself not only in the good times but in the absolute worst times as well. Beckham informed us that his goal was to play in the World Cup, and that he wasn't going to accept the traditional recovery timeline: he wanted to be completely healed and ready for play in six months. With this dream fully visualized and articulated, he commanded his journey.

He set a course of progressive improvement with small and large goals. Although he wasn't ready for the 2010 World Cup, he returned to play much faster than anyone expected after a ruptured Achilles. The LA Galaxy won the 2011 MLS Cup in what was Beckham's best season ever; he accomplished that feat again in 2012.

There was another moment to watch the "mend it like Beckham" magic work even beyond the two championships with the LA Galaxy. This one was not so pretty or kind. Beckham was part of the bid committee for the 2012 Summer Olympics in London, and part of the fiber of British soccer, but the coach did not select him for the Olympic team. Many people, and especially Beckham, were disappointed and amazed that he was left off the squad. But in typical classy Beckham form, he held his head high, with a smile on his face, and persevered as usual, becoming a star of the opening Olympic ceremonies and the face of the London Olympic Games. Not making the team could've bummed him out, but he wouldn't let that happen. He applied the victorious spirit off the field, inspiring every Olympic spectator.

THE US SABER TEAM: ALWAYS SET A BIGGER GOAL

The US has never been commended for its fencing. Unlike the European powerhouses whose competitors are recognized and revered, the US pays very little attention to this Olympic sport. Many do not even know that such a team exists.

Despite a respectable showing in Athens in 2004, the men's fencing team lost to Russia in the semifinals, one point away from bronze. Their proximity to medal recognition ignited a fire that drove them to train even harder for Beijing.

By late 2007, Keeth Smart and Tim Morehouse rose to #1 and #2 in the US respectively and were ranked in the top ten internationally. While the rest of the world denigrated Morehouse's fencing, his clunky, unconventional way proved successful as his confidence in his contrarian style grew. Smart, on the other hand, was the consummate athlete, an impeccable strategist. He moved with such art and craft on the strip that he neared perfection as the closer, whose role was to bring it all home in team play.

Alongside these two men were Jason Rogers and James Williams. Rogers, winning his way onto the team in one match at the Nationals, and Williams, grabbing the alternate spot as a mathematical long shot, added to the unlikely athletes who made up the US Saber Team. Due to their previous nearness to victory, the team set a goal: win a medal in the team event.

Tied with Hungary 44–44 in the quarterfinals, the team found themselves in a precarious position. It all fell on Smart to get that last point. It was his moment—a moment that would define his career.

Instead of lunging at his opponent like he normally would do, he hung back, baiting his Hungarian competitor Zsolt Nemcsik. The Hungarian took it, and approached, attacking. In that split second, the Hungarian stabbed Smart, but only after the American had landed a touch on his wrist. It was only the second team win over Hungary in US history.

The next hurdle came against Russia, who, like Hungary, the US had only beaten once before. After close battles for Rogers and Williams, once again the pressure lay on the shoulders of Smart. While he had taken eight points to the Russian's four, it was far from enough. He had fought back to a close 44–43, but he was still down with one point ending the team's hopes for a medal.

An awkward misstep, and the Russian Stanislav Pozdnyakov scored. Smart hung his head, and the team saw their dreams disappear. All of a sudden, the referee gathered the other officials around the replay machine. After a painstaking ten minutes, the call was in—a dead point. Smart still had a chance!

Reinvigorated with hope, Smart scored. The opponents were tied. Retreating back past his own starting line, Smart saw the hesitation in the Russian's eyes: Should he follow Smart down the strip? Keeth scored the next two touches and the US advanced to the gold medal bout for the first time in Men's Sabre. In a miraculous eight-foot leap into a flying lunge, Smart pulled off the impossible and scored the winning point.

Smart had outscored Pozdnyakov, a man with more World Championships than anyone in the history of the weapon, an incredible 10–4. Uncontrollably jubilant, the team hugged and cried. They had achieved their goal.

But their journey wasn't over yet. With a chance at gold, they were so distracted by their semifinal win that let them place, that they lost focus in the finals, competing against France. They were never really in it. All they had aimed to do was place. They never set a goal beyond the finish line.

Losing to France 45–37, the US Men's Saber Team had not set their bar high enough. With their dreams already met, they didn't pursue more in the finals. The US Men's Saber Team had found the victorious spirit within them; yet they lost it psychologically when they didn't set their goals high enough.

CHARLIE DAVIES:
A COMEBACK OF BODY AND SPIRIT

It's late at night. I'm talking to an emergency room physician on the East Coast who I'd trained with decades before at Shock-Trauma in Baltimore. He'd just come out of the operating room with a "John Doe" brought in from a catastrophic car accident. But it's no John Doe—it's Charlie Davies, a young star with the US Men's Soccer Team, at the height of his career.

This talented athlete—who seemed almost invincible—had demonstrated the kind of bad judgment that night that many of us do once or twice in life. We don't always pay a price. But sometimes we do. Unfortunately for Davies, it went very badly.

The night of October 13, 2009, was supposed to be one of celebration. The US Men's Soccer Team was better than ever, and the team was in Washington, DC, to play a qualifier against Costa Rica the next night. In a fairytale of a game a few months before, the US had beaten top-ranked Spain to finish in second place at the 2009 Confederations Cup in South Africa. Star striker Davies and his teammates had everything going for them. But one bad decision and an unlucky twist of fate made it all come crashing down for Davies.

That night before the game, he decided to go out after curfew. After meeting up with two friends, he got in the car with them to drive back to their hotel. They never made it. The driver lost control on the George Washington Parkway. The car hit a guardrail and split in half. One passenger was killed instantly when she was thrown from the car. The driver left the scene without any serious injuries. Davies was not so lucky. Though he was miraculously not killed like his fellow passenger, he was pinned inside the vehicle and suffered horrible injuries.

Davies was rushed to the hospital with broken bones in his legs and face, bleeding in his brain, a broken elbow, and a lacerated bladder. Davies entered the emergency room as a "John Doe," and the doctors had no idea that they were treating one of the best soccer players in the country. The trauma doctor was shocked when the young patient's identity was confirmed. The tragedy of the situation set in: Davies, a young athlete with so much promise, would never play the same way again.

In addition to all the physical rehab that he would have to go through, Davies had to come to terms with his actions on that fateful night. He regretted making the decision to break team curfew. He felt awful for letting his team, his family, and his fans down. He had let himself down too, and in the process, he learned that he was not invincible. Basketball coach John Wooden said it best: "It is best not to drink too deeply from a cup full of fame. It can be intoxicating, and intoxicated people often do foolish things."[6]

Davies would have a lot of work to do himself, but a great athlete is nothing without his supporters, and the outpouring of love from the people who cared about him was, without question, a crucial part of his recovery. His family and his teammates supported him as he overcame his injuries. His loyal fiancée, Nina Stavris, stayed by his side.

One of the most stunning displays of support for Davies came in the wake of the tragedy. The day after the accident, the US Men's Soccer Team stepped out onto the turf at RFK Stadium to play Costa Rica. Word had spread about the horrific accident. The US supporters in the crowd came prepared with their red #9 jerseys and big signs, sharing with the team their hope that Davies would make a full recovery. The spirit of the fans that day helped the Americans carry on without their teammate. The game against Costa Rica ended in a tie, an acceptable finish for a team in shock, but the US would have to gather some more strength before the World Cup tournament began. Davies would not see footage of this game until days after the accident. He knew that he should have been there, and that his teammates had needed him. It was a lot to wrap his head around.

Fortunately, Davies realized that he couldn't change the past, so he instead dedicated himself to the future. He warned others against making the choices he made, which could have led to more serious injuries, or even death. But the only way Davies could totally redeem himself was to get through rehab, get back in the game, and be just as good a player as he was before.

But for Davies, getting back on the field was never out of the question. He came to Los Angeles two months after the accident, as I was supervising his rehabilitation. He came into the room and when I asked him how he was feeling, he said, "Doc, I feel great!" Then he began to jog in place. This was an amazing moment for me, one that almost brought tears to my eyes. It was one of the most powerful examples of the triumphant spirit that I had ever seen. Eight weeks prior, this young man was in the emergency room with broken bones and an uncertain, improbable future. Now, the bones were healed and he was on his feet again. As a doctor, I could see that Davies would, without a doubt, walk again and lead a normal life.

But, I knew that he had a long road ahead of him if he wanted to get back onto the field. The 2010 World Cup was approaching and Davies was in pretty rough shape. Many major surgeries were required to rebuild his body. He had to have titanium rods inserted into his broken femur and tibia bones, as well as plates and screws in his elbow and face. Doctors repaired his bladder. His recovery was expected to take anywhere between six months and a whole year. Davies's strong, fit body would make recovery achievable, but it still wouldn't be easy.

In my medical career, I had seen a couple of athletes sustain serious injuries like these, and only a few of them recovered enough to return to true competitive sport. It would take a strong effort, both physically and mentally, but Davies was determined to be back on the field for the World Cup.

With the support of his family, friends, and fans around him, Davies began to rebuild his athletic career. He knew that he would have to go step by step to get better. The first step was getting back on his feet. His broken leg would make things difficult, in spite of his certainty that he would succeed in getting his strength back. The break in his femur was healing, but it still gave him a considerable amount of pain when he started rehab. Davies felt down on his luck for a while, but when the pain subsided, his self-esteem went up. Thanks to special exercise equipment and a great big dose of determination, he was making progress.

But, would it be enough to make the national team for the World Cup? That part of his future was still uncertain, but Davies sure hoped so. He felt ready to play again. By early 2010, he was jogging and working out. In March, Davies began training with Sochaux, his soccer club in France.

While Davies was recovering extremely well, US coach Bob Bradley announced that Davies would not be on the US roster because he was not medically cleared by Sochaux and, therefore, would not go to the World Cup. Davies was heartbroken. He worked so hard, faced incredible odds, and now his shot at this World Cup was gone.

Even though his year didn't work out the way he wanted it to, Davies didn't go through everything he had for nothing. It was time for him to move on—there would be plenty more World Cups in his bright future, and his journey from this point forward would be rewarding no matter what happened.

In early 2011, Davies did very well in a ten-day trial for soccer club D.C. United and was loaned to D.C. for a year by Sochaux. It was here where he made his huge comeback.

He wasn't playing as well as he had before the accident, but what improvements he'd made were promising and inspiring. His speed was improving, his skills were getting sharper, and critics were becoming more and more convinced that Davies would be playing like his old self again. By the end of his time with D.C. United, he had scored eleven goals for his team, and even though he wasn't signed to the team at the end of the year, it was still a big step in Davies's post-accident career. Since then, Davies's life has been going uphill. In the summer of 2012, Davies happily announced that he would begin playing for Denmark soccer club Randers FC, where he hoped he could really get back into the game. The same summer, he also married his fiancée, Nina. Who would have thought that, just three years after a near-death experience, Davies would be so blessed? Then again, good things come to those who work hard and keep their spirits up!

No one, not even an all-star athlete, is immune to tragedy, but even those of us who aren't all-star athletes can overcome the disasters that threaten our lives. No one, myself included, ever thought Charlie Davies would play at a high level after that accident, but because of his strong will throughout the rehab process, he exceeded our expectations and is back on track in his career.

Sometimes we do things we aren't proud of. The night of Davies's accident demonstrates that. He wasn't proud of his behavior, and he wished he'd acted differently. But we are all human and we all make mistakes. Every day we make decisions and not all of them are good ones. But no good ever comes of dwelling on our mistakes, since we can't change the past. The best we can do is move on with our lives and try to better ourselves. We just have to remember that even the best of us have very low lows. The important thing is that we keep participating in the sport of life, keep striving to be the best we can. That's what finding the win within is all about.

• • •

These stories amaze us, due to the level of spirit these individuals showed. Despite adversity, they held on to their ambitious demands, and to their spirit and passion, leaving the world in awe at their success.

A broken leg is for many the end of a career, not the beginning of a journey back to the Olympics. But this is the heart of the matter: it is the spirit within that drives the outer being. The individuals discussed in this chapter have mastered this inner victorious spirit and now find their lives blessed.

That does not mean that they do not face adversity and trial, but they have the spirit to fight against it. They have the strength to say, "These are my dreams! Why live if I abandon them in difficulty? That is when they need me the most." Have you ever said those words? Have you ever accessed the victorious spirit within? Because here's the secret: it's resting within you, right at this very moment. Take a page from Davies's book: Your situation will not change unless you put in a good effort to change it. You'll never know unless you try.

Beckham ruptured his Achilles tendon and was back on the field in only six months. Daggett approached the comeback from his broken leg, not as the end of a career, but as the beginning of a new dream and road back to the Olympics. And Davies created a new game plan and refused to be devoured by or defined by his worst moment. How were they able to perform these acts of grandeur and greatness and amaze the public through the drive of their dreams? They didn't let others tell them what they could or could not do. They didn't let failure stop them short, and they didn't allow society, danger, culture, science, or even nature to put a stop to their inner dreams. In a sense, their very commitment enabled and sanctioned their dreams.

The spirit that drives a dream or goal is everything. Though the spirit can't be defined—and manifests itself in varying ways—it retains certain common characteristics: passion, adaptability, realistic optimism, and a refusal to accept mediocrity.

The stories in this chapter are examples of how the spirit can be accessed as a superpower, beyond physical prowess. In fact, the greatest powers of the athletes discussed in this chapter were asserted when their exemplary physical strength was stressed. It's beautiful that they held on to their spirit and passion and executed a practice and plan that left the world in awe of their heroic efforts and journeys.

Athletes offer us permission to believe in and pursue unlikely or improbable goals and dreams. They motivate us to do the hard work, to perseverance, and to evolve. Their victorious spirit is in all of us—it's not just reserved for elite athletes. It's something that can be summoned and leveraged with practice and the right tools. We all have the ability to transform misfortune into victory.

CHAPTER 3

The Collective Victorious Spirit

A SOLITARY HORSEMAN ILLUMINATED BY A single shimmering spotlight enters the Olympic stadium at the 2000 Summer Olympics in Sydney. He marches forward to the theme from the film *The Man from Snowy River*. As the light focuses the attention of the world on the horse and rider, I am distracted by the remembrance of a patient's shared confidences from a few days earlier. This individual was not just a patient but also a friend.

Three days ago, I was summoned to Clive Charles's temporary office in Sydney. Nothing out of the ordinary: he is the coach of the US Men's Soccer Team and I am their physician. I anticipated a conversation about a practice injury or a preventative measure that should be implemented to prevent one. Instead, I went from the intense sunlight of Sydney at midday to the dimly lit confines of Clive's make-do office. We normally begin a conversation with friendly banter—something about the inconveniences of travel, details about our families, the weather, the stats, etc.—but this time was different. I knew from the minute I stepped over the threshold. With my eyes on his troubled face, I sat down in the chair opposite his small desk without saying a word. His eyes were downcast and locked on a folded piece of paper floating loosely in his fingers.

Clive was a soccer player. Born in London, he began his career early, playing with teams in London, Montreal, and Cardiff City, where he was captain. In the late seventies, Clive came to the United States and signed with the Portland Timbers, where he played for three seasons. After a year of indoor soccer, split between Pittsburgh and Los Angeles, and three years of coaching at the high school level, Clive returned to Portland as coach of the University of Portland Men's—and later Women's—Soccer Teams. He went on to coach at the international level with the US Under-20 Women's, US Under-23 Men's, and US Men's teams. He was a teacher of many and a friend to all.

"I have six months to live," he blankly stated. "I have been diagnosed with metastatic prostate cancer." A week earlier, they had found blood in his urine biopsy. Our eyes slowly filled with tears as we talked together. We cried together. I promised Clive that his condition would remain strictly private information.

The tears had barely dried before we had to put on our game faces. There were matches to be played. Battles to be won. Medals to be earned. Clive's priority was the athletes and the game, not his illness. I had to do the same—not only out of respect for Clive but also for my own sanity.

I look out over the buzzing crowd. My seat in the stands of the Olympic stadium is high enough that I actually have a better view than many of the people who are in the lower premium seats. As much of the action takes place mid-air during this opening ceremony, being seated higher is a great advantage. I tell my brain to put the grief aside and be in the Olympic moment.

Surgeons are accustomed to tragedy—but you never get used to it. I don't know any physician who has been able to extinguish the empathy felt for a patient consumed with pain or one who has no future. I have the great fortune to provide medical care for some of the finest athletes in the world—athletes who are respected by millions for their extraordinary gifts. I force myself to engage with the spectacle going on around me.

A giant banner hangs high in the stadium and greets the world with "G'Day." Soon the lone horse and rider are joined by a hundred or so others marching in precision to form the five Olympic rings in the finale. This symbol represents the coming together of athletes from the five continents of the world. Leaving behind social, economic, and political differences, these contestants represent the best that their country has to offer. They compete for the glory of their nation and are on the quest for personal victory that lies in the heart of every elite athlete.

The stadium transforms into an ocean. Colorful sea creatures scurry across the glistening ocean floor toward the enormous pink jellyfish drifting gracefully overhead. Their tentacles dance to the magnificent symphony, which provides the infrastructure for this grand oceanic production. Acrobatic swimmers join the scene, which is a tribute to the Great Barrier Reef. Australia's aboriginal past is recognized and celebrated, as an Aboriginal elder leads an Australian pop singer through an awakening. The flora and fauna of the continent explode into view, serenaded sweetly by dreamy music and children's voices. The special effects, the dancers in brilliantly lit luminescent costumes, and the staggering number of performers—estimated at twelve thousand—take my breath away as I surrender to the wonder of this brilliantly coordinated performance.

The mood shifts from the natural beauty and grandeur of the Australian wilderness to the contemporary music culture as the two-thousand-strong Millennium Marching Band enters the stadium. Six conductors are required to keep the live performance in sync and playing as one voice. The Parade of Nations begins. Each of the International Olympic Committee members has sent a delegation, with the exception of Afghanistan. Of great significance is the fact that the athletes from North and South Korea are marching under a single unified flag, although they will compete separately. Four athletes from East Timor march under the Olympic flag because the International Olympic Committee does not yet recognize their emerging country.

It is a humbling experience to see the pride and the thrill that these young people feel as they walk across the world's stage as the designated representatives of their native, or in some cases adopted, country. Through the years, I have learned that each athlete in this stadium has an extraordinary story: many having overcome seemingly insurmountable odds to march in this parade. Their personal stories include all types of adversity—financial, political, religious, cultural, physical, and sometimes medical. As the team from each member nation enters the stadium, a swell of cheers and applause momentarily overwhelms the music. Friends and compatriots celebrate the accomplishments of the athletes and demonstrate the extent of their patriotic fervor through the energy and volume of their exuberance. In these dramatic moments, the citizens celebrate as one, putting aside local differences and internal rivalries.

As a member of the audience, yet nonetheless a part of these Olympics, my heart swells with gratitude as I reflect on my own great fortune to have been selected to be a physician for these extraordinary athletes.

The parade is led by the delegation from Greece, in recognition of the sponsorship of the original Olympic Games in 776 BC. The parade is customarily concluded with the march of the delegation from the host country. In between, the nations march in alphabetical order (according to the English alphabet) wearing carefully designed costumes that express the colors or the cultural uniqueness of the country. Because of my participation on the medical staff of several international sports teams, I know personally several individuals from countries other than my own. When my friends march, many of them former patients, I cheer as loudly as I can in honor of their achievement.

Roughly a full hour goes by before the team from the United States enters the stadium. I have a special interest in the parade of US athletes, transcending my own nationalistic pride. It is a long-standing Olympic custom for the delegation to elect one of its members to bear the flag during the march, and it is an extraordinary honor to be selected by your teammates to be the flag bearer. It is often done in recognition of some extraordinary achievement or special circumstance. When the US team entered the stadium that special night in Sydney, I surrendered to the force of emotions that had been welling up inside of me all week. As Cliff Meidl took those first few steps into the stadium, I was overcome with an unexplainable mix of tragedy, grief, irony, and joy.

Fourteen years earlier, Cliff lay dying on an emergency room table having taken thirty thousand volts of electricity through his body. Typically, when a convicted criminal is being put to death in an electric chair, fifteen hundred to two thousand volts are applied to carry out the purpose. Cliff, then a twenty-year-old construction worker, was working on a job site when his jackhammer hit three high voltage electrical cables. The surge was so powerful that it shot outward from within his body, resulting in the literal explosion of his interior constitution. His body immediately went into shock. His heart stopped. Paramedics arrived and performed CPR. His heart started again, and he was rushed to the emergency room. Three times during the race to the hospital, he was resuscitated by the astonishing efforts of the emergency personnel.

Dr. Malcolm Lesavoy, a plastic surgeon I had previously worked with on a number of occasions, brought me into the emergency room. I was an attending physician one year out of fellowship. I had several years of residency, which trained me to operate on the worst imaginable traumas. No one had imagined a thirty-thousand-volt electrical shock. Nothing had prepared me for what I saw.

I walked into the trauma room and saw Cliff terrified and in excruciating pain. He had endured three cardiac arrests, burns covering over 15 percent of his body, an exploded shoulder blade, and a head injury that we were still trying to assess. But his knee joints suffered the primary damage, as the electricity had burned away over a third of their internal structure, disintegrating them completely.

The team of physicians, including myself, anticipated a great deal of work, but I already knew that Cliff would put forth the most arduous effort. Our first concern was preventing amputation. There was little likelihood that Cliff would ever walk again, but saving his legs remained the top priority. Along with Dr. Lesavoy, I began reconstructing his legs and knees. Cliff underwent a total of fifteen surgeries over the next three and a half years.

We sent him home from the hospital with a wheelchair. He never used it. I supervised his rehabilitation and met with him for postoperative assessments of his condition. Each time he came in for a checkup, I was amazed. His strides in physical rehabilitation, as profound as they were, were not the cause of my astonishment. It was his unwavering spirit that impressed me above all else. With every visit, Cliff seemed more and more determined to progress with his healing and reclaim his vitality. Every challenge, every step in this long and painful recovery, was met with "No problem," "I can do this," "What's next?," and "I can—I can and will walk again, I will become whole!" He took every step with a steadfast eye on the prize, always with a smile, always wanting more, and never once complaining. All those around him could sense his confidence, optimism, and positivity. There was something that was so intuitively unique and empowering for him. He truly had a *higher* calling. And it was!

During his demanding and seemingly overwhelming rehab, he resumed canoeing—an interest he had before the accident. Already an athletic individual, his upper body strength increased dramatically from his therapy and prolonged use of crutches. He had almost instant proficiency in rowing. As the months went by, he switched to kayaking, a sport he could participate in which did not require the use of his legs. Cliff grew in both spirit and confidence through his new hobby, challenging himself daily with an incessant push for progression. Rather than submit to defeat, Cliff harnessed the physical and emotional trauma of his accident as a fuel for a new internal fire.

Cliff began racing competitively and soon achieved national recognition. He won several national titles and qualified for the US Men's Kayak Team in the 1996 Summer Olympics in Atlanta. Less than ten years had passed since his brush with death and he now stood among the world's finest athletes. Like most Olympians, Cliff set his sights on future goals, persisting in his dedication to the sport and striving to make the US Men's Kayak Team in 2000. Cliff had set his goal, executed his plan, and made the team.

As I watched him carry our country's colors into the Olympic stadium, I recalled his lifeless body in the emergency room. We had reconstructed his legs using muscle tissue and local flaps from his calf, and we had taken skin grafts from his thighs. Marching with a normal gait and a broad grin, no one would suspect that it took Cliff thousands of hours and unimaginable pain to rebuild and restrengthen his body. Just his normal gait and broad grin overtook me with emotion. Pride radiated from him as he held the flag high in his magnificent arms and marched on the medical miracle that were his legs.

Reflecting on this beautiful man consumed with happiness, bursting with life, my mind flashed to Clive, who was clinging to his last days. Clive's admission into treatment, paired with Cliff's star-spangled triumph, encompassed all of life's complexity. The glow of vitality, the light of their lives, reflected even brighter against the darkness of their adversities. The journey made by these two heroes, replayed against the backdrop of the ceremony's lights, music, dance, and technical effects, was more than I could bear. I could no longer suppress the overwhelming flow of emotions. I cried. I laughed. I felt all of life's brilliance and tragedy in one moment on this opening night of the Sydney Olympics. I stood at the crossroads of life and death, witnessing the synchrony of adversity and triumph, in awe of the victorious Olympic spirit within.

In that moment, I felt that everyone in that ceremony—and everyone watching around the world—had been united in this momentary Olympic experience, all of us inspiring each other to ever-greater heights, daring each other to dream ever-greater dreams. This is one of the beautiful things about the win within: it can be a collective experience in which seemingly disparate groups gathered together in one collective "arena" become jointly inspired by the spectacle of the victorious spirit. Nowhere is this more apparent than at the Olympic Games.

THE OLYMPIC SPIRIT

Dare to dream: this challenge encompasses the underlying spirit of every Olympic Games, from the lighting of the flame to its quenching. From the time of the ancient Greeks to that of Cathy Freeman and Muhammad Ali in the Atlanta Olympic Games of 1996, the traditions established at the games' inception have evolved. While the Greek origins may seem distant or dated in comparison to today's grandiose, commercial spectacle, the core values of the competition have remained untouched by the passage of time.

Just as in the games of ancient Greece, where quarrels among city-states were postponed for the duration of the competition, today's games prioritize the suspension of cultural and sociopolitical differences in order to highlight the global commonality of the human passion for sport. This environment of international unity allows each participant to cultivate and express his or her Olympic spirit, the Promethean fire that fuels competition, achievement, and advancement.

The games glorify the potential for human greatness and the human capacity to redefine the bounds of greatness. "*Citius, Altius, Fortius*": Faster, Higher, Stronger. These words, the motto of the Olympic Games since 1894, greatly exceed their physical connotations. They capture the primal spirit, the unceasing thirst for betterment that evolution has carved into our genetics.

The Olympic spirit is measured not by the athletes' statistical accomplishment, but by their drive, their stamina, and their unwavering confrontation with adversity. Perseverance remains at the core of this spirit. The games are a time of the highest highs of relentless determination in the athletes' preparation and passion in their action. They merge the physical, emotional, mental, and spiritual elements of human life, a crossroads of dreams and realities.

The Olympics allow for expression of the human passion that resides, too often dormant, in every moment of life, from the monumental, to the mundane. We watch the games not as spectators but as fellow participants in our hearts. We indulge the fantasy that we have something great in us. The athletes we idolize are masters of the same internal fire that you and I possess. In every facet of life, there is an opportunity to assert the Olympic spirit—the victorious spirit—to push for achievement previously not thought possible and dare to dream.

It has been the promise of witnessing human success that has made the games so popular. Spectators watch in awe of the sweat, the discipline, the hard work, and the drive of the athletes. They see raw human emotion in its most rare form. The Olympics has become not just a gathering of locals but a coming together every four years of the entire world to witness the power of athletic competition. There is a power and a privilege in realizing that we are attracted to sport not just as spectacle but as a motivator and as an inspiration for life. Spectator and participant, we are drawn to the activity, the action, the drama, and the impact this has on our world. Events like this allow the public to realize what we saw in Chapter 1: human beings, at our core, have a vigorous athletic spirit built into our DNA.

Through Olympics and international sports, we understand and highlight the features that are similar between human beings, and we understand better how to celebrate and embrace our differences. The palpable emotions of the games are primal and universally motivating for each athlete, official, fan, and participant. They transcend the thrill of victory and the excitement of winning. They illuminate the intense human spirit, the thin line between winning and losing, and the drama of injury, fatigue, or the fall. They emphasize both the imperfections and perfections at the highest level. They provide a contagious lift to the self-consciousness and self-esteem of all involved. This is this high that we all pursue, whether we know it consciously or not. It is part of our human hardwiring to discover, anticipate, and master the athlete inside each of us. Just watch how it makes you feel: the warmth, the goose bumps, the smile, the tears. These feelings are inextricably linked to our human spirit and dreams.

The games' ability to bring a group of people together and create a sense of community is what makes them so special and unique. No matter the political views of the countries involved, no matter the religion or race of the participants, nations proudly come together in a collective spirit for their athletes.

The human being is drawn to share in the magical event that personifies these symbols and then internalizes these symbols in an intense passion for this collective human event. It is compelling, motivating, and inspiring for all. It is here that we discover the most basic of human passions—the victorious spirit. The values of the Olympic spirit are hard work, perseverance, and competition alongside the drama, the story, the music, the scent, the crowd, and the raw emotions. It's during individual events that you can look past the games and into the heart of the athletes and truly see their greatness. These superheroes have the ability to sustain a goal over a long duration. The journey may be tortuous, but the destination is never in question.

Their greatness, their stamina, and their drive are what make up the Olympic spirit, and it is what releases the victorious spirit. It's the highest of the high, the human pinnacle of intense joy and emotion, the merging of the spiritual, the physical, the emotional, and the cognitive. It's the crossroads of hopes, dreams, and hard work.

HOW THE OLYMPIC GAMES CAME TO BE

When Baron Pierre de Coubertin wanted to reestablish the Olympic tradition, he had hundreds of years to draw upon for inspiration and thought. Believed to have begun in the year 776 BC, the first Olympic competition consisted of a single event: a foot race of one stadion, which is about 190 meters. "Stadion" is the root of a word we now often use in sports, "stadium." Competitors ran nude, in honor of the gods and to revel in the beauty of the male figure. Koroibos, a local baker, championed the race. Awarded with an olive branch wreath, Koroibos was the world's first to bask in the esteem and self-satisfaction of an Olympic victory, setting the bar for centuries of future contestants.[7]

Like many of the common events among the Greek people, the Olympic Games were steeped in religion. Many myths surround their initial creation, but the essential idea was this: competing at a high athletic level honored the gods and brought peace to the nations. We can see this philosophy echoed in the games today.

The ancient Olympic Games generally focused on foot and horse racing, but other events eventually came into being: boxing, wrestling, and the ancient pentathlon, which consisted of javelin, long jump, discus, wrestling, and a stadion.

The games made heroic legends out of local laymen for over a millennium. However, in 393 AD, the Roman emperor Theodosius abolished them. He believed that their contents conflicted with his stern

Christian morality and deemed them nothing more than a pagan ritual. The ban endured for 1,500 years.

In the late nineteenth century, Pierre de Coubertin, a French historian and professor, had the vision to restore the centuries-lost tradition of celebrating athletic pride. Now considered the father of the modern Olympic Games, de Coubertin, harkening back to the athletic ideals of antiquity, became interested in the interrelatedness of athletics, education, character development, and politics. He found further inspiration through his relationships with two prominent figures: Thomas Arnold and Dr. William Penny Brookes.

Captivated by *Tom Brown's School Days*, Thomas Hughes's novel about a youth's experience in a rugby academy, de Coubertin sought out the source of his intrigue and traveled to England, where he met Thomas Arnold. De Coubertin admired Arnold, headmaster of the United Kingdom's prominent Rugby School, as one of the founders of what he termed "athletic chivalry." Arnold's pioneering of physical education as a source of moral growth resonated with de Coubertin's own beliefs, reinforced by the latter's meetings with Dr. William Penny Brookes.

Brookes, an English surgeon, botanist, and educator, found athletic activity to be a catalyst not only for personal physical health but for social well-being as well. In 1850, in the town of Much Wenlock situated in central Shropshire, he founded the concept of "Olympic Class" that evolved to the Wenlock Olympic Games. Inspired by Arnold's philosophy of athletics as morally enriching, and Brookes's belief in social cohesion through competition, de Coubertin returned to France determined to renew the Olympic spirit.

After several failed attempts to integrate an improved system of athletics à la Arnold into the French educational system, de Coubertin redirected his focus toward a revival of the ancient Greek games, picking up where Brookes left off. He established the International Olympic Committee in 1894 and organized its first Olympic Games in 1896, appropriately held in Athens, Greece. Except for a few fledgling local competitions, his was the first revival of the Greek tradition and the first-ever Olympic competition held on a truly international scale. The global public received this first reincarnation only tepidly, as they did the 1900 Summer Olympics in Paris, which was overshadowed by the World's Fair. Unmoved by the threat of discontinuation, de Coubertin refused to compromise his belief in the games' importance and planned vigorously for the 1904 Summer Olympics in St. Louis.

Despite their sluggish start, the Olympics continued to gain the interest of the public as a result of the tremendous feats of the athletes. England's Charlotte Cooper shattered the games' gender barrier by winning the tennis singles in 1900. German-American gymnast George Eyser won six medals in one day during the 1904 Games. He wore a wooden prosthesis as one of his legs.

De Coubertin fully understood the Olympics' capacity to congregate nations, to highlight the passion and innovation of national heroes, to relay the inspiration that they provide to the global public, and to create legendary performances that inspire all of us. And as mentioned at the outset of this book, he stated that "the important thing about the Olympic Games is not the winning but the taking part . . . the essential thing in life is not conquering but fighting well." He understood that the games had the potential to inspire everyone: all the competitors, whether they won or not, and all the spectators, who were moved by the spectacle of elite athleticism and this ancient spirit.

The efforts of de Coubertin and Brookes to create the games were never forgotten. In his speech at the opening ceremony of the 2012 Summer Olympics in London, International Olympic Committee president Dr. Jacques Rogge praised the 30th Olympiad's host country for combining sports, education, and hope for the future throughout its history. "It was here that the concepts of sportsmanship and fair play were first codified into clear rules and regulations. It was here that sport was included as an educational tool in the school curriculum," Rogge told the millions of people listening. "The British approach to sport had a profound influence on Pierre de Coubertin, our founder, as he developed the framework for the modern Olympic movement at the close of the nineteenth century. The values that inspired de Coubertin will come to life over the next seventeen days as the world's best athletes compete in a spirit of friendship, respect, and fair play."[8]

Though he wasn't named, this speech honored Brookes's belief in the connection between sports and a healthy, productive society, and assured us that the Brookes and de Coubertin visions live on today.

THE SPIRIT OF HUMAN TRIUMPH

In 2000, at the conclusion of the Parade of Nations, John Farnham and Olivia Newton-John took the stage to sing a song written especially for the ceremony, "Dare to Dream,"[9] a refrain that has become a rallying cry for Olympians. More than ten thousand athletes from 199 national Olympic teams stood on the field that night, listening to words that articulated their own extraordinary quest: they had all dared to dream, they all had been chosen, and each embodied the strength to transcend limitations so the spirit could soar.

Following the tradition, the opening ceremony concluded with the lighting of the Olympic flame. The roots of the ritual lie in ancient Greek culture: Greeks revered fire as a symbol of divine power. The ancient lighting of the flame celebrated the myth of Prometheus, the Titan who boldly stole Zeus's precious fire and bequeathed it to humans. A treasure previously relegated only to the gods, the gift of fire sparked the ignition of all human progression. We became gods in our abilities; earth became our Mount Olympus. The Olympic flame now burns throughout the games in commemoration of human triumph. It honors past sacrifices, showcases present successes, and forecasts future glories.

In Sydney's ceremony in 2000, the lighting took place in celebration of the one hundred years of women's participation in the games. A succession of Australia's greatest living female athletes carried the torch through the stadium, finally handing it to Cathy Freeman, an Aborigine who had been named "Australian of the Year" two years prior. Freeman, a skilled sprinter, would go on to win gold in the games' 400-meter dash. Torch in hand, she climbed a steep flight of stairs to a circular pond. She waded into the pond and lit the cauldron, surrounding her in a ring of fire. The flaming cauldron then rose around and above the statuesque Freeman and, after a brief technical delay, began its mechanical ascension toward the crest of the massive stadium. Reaching the apex of its course, the cauldron's blaze was accompanied by an enormous fireworks display. Light consumed the stadium—the glare of the flame, the glow of the fireworks, the endless flicker of camera flashes, and brightest of all, the radiant smiles on the upturned faces of the athletes and spectators. Let the games begin!

In moments like these, the collective victorious spirit buoys us up, motivating and inspiring us to accomplish great things in the future. But this sense of triumph and pride—and the unification it brings—becomes all the more important when unimaginable tragedy strikes.

COMING TOGETHER TO FACE THE UNTHINKABLE

The day was September 11, 2001, and I'd been invited to be a keynote speaker at the Youth Soccer World Cup Conference in Port of Spain, Trinidad and Tobago. At precisely 8:50 a.m. Eastern Standard Time I walked into the lobby of the Hilton Hotel with my computer in arm. Ready to speak, I looked up at the big-screen TV and saw the second airplane strike the World Trade Center. My knees weakened as my stomach soured and I tried to focus my brain on what had transpired. What happened? Who could possibly do this? And why? Alone, I stood 3,924 miles from home as the unthinkable events unfolded: as a terrorist attack rocked our world and 2,996 people perished[10]—the buildings crashing down, thousands dead, some holding on to precious moments, others leaping to their certain death. It was all unfolding: the worst nightmare of death and the fear of losing one of our loved ones in this maelstrom. At that moment, my good friend, and the only other American at our event, Hank Steinbrecher, former general secretary of US Soccer, found me and we watched, hugged, and cried.

We spent the next five days supporting each other, as flying home was not an available option. I tried over and over to leave, but our nation's airline industry was grounded. Hank's son Chad, a Navy SEAL, emailed us from an unknown location, responding to the tragedy with a sense of resolve and focused determination: "We will survive, we will endure, and we will thrive. We will be victorious!" This same spirit resonated in the country and the world in response to this devastating act of terror that had changed life as we know it eternally.

Post-9/11, in June of 2002, the US World Cup Soccer Team was the first American "asset" to venture to a global event not on our soil. As the team doctor, we had to prepare differently for this World Cup. We flew to New York and were hosted by the firefighters as we toured ground zero. The enormity of the hole, the remnants, the Survivor Tree, and the stories riveted each of us as we absorbed the devastation of this event. We hugged, cried, and stood with resolve. We understood the bigger picture, as this was the intersection between sport and life, and life and sports, and we were determined to be victorious as a team and as a people. The words of Chad Steinbrecher—"We will be victorious!"—reverberated as we flew to Seoul.

The minute our plane landed, I saw that things would be different now that 9/11 had happened. On the tarmac, our plane was surrounded by military vehicles and tanks; four Chinook helicopters circled above us. The South Korean and American soldiers formed a surrounding column as we walked from the plane to the bus. Next to the bus tanks stood with turrets aimed and readied, and helicopters hovered above us. The sounds, sights, and reality of what we were entering were on the scale of a Jack Ryan action movie. We were there for a game, but this was not just about sport. Our brains and hearts tried to comprehend what was occurring, what could occur, and what our mission was. At that moment, I asked one of the twenty-five CIA agents sitting next to me, "What is happening?" He responded in a very calm and deliberate manner: "There is a clear and present danger."

The team traveled to the practice field daily with protective American helicopters overhead and with the CIA agents monitoring for chemical, biological, and radiation sensors around the field. In spite of the disastrous potential events and the pressures of the World Cup, the team responded with an unprecedented "game face" and historic results, only losing to Germany in the quarterfinals (the round of eight). As I watched these results, I realized that a powerful force had transformed this team of athletes and staff—the collective victorious spirit.

Over ten years later, I'd see this force at work again. On April 15, 2013, the world watched once again as the unthinkable occurred, this time at the Boston Marathon. It was four hours, ten minutes, and forty-five seconds into the event when two well-planned and sequenced sloppy bombs ignited death and devastation at the finish line. With the detonation came a wave of terrorism resulting in eardrums exploding and shrapnel penetrating limbs, causing horrifying bleeding, trauma, and loss of life. Probably the largest team of emergency medical personnel at any athletic event in history leaped into action, prepared for the worst. They were able to save life and limb.

I am sure that the terrorists considered how significant and iconic the finish line of a marathon is and, in specific, the finish line of the Boston Marathon—iconic, deeply American, the best of the best. But, this highly symbolic act of terror did not break our spirits. At this terrible moment, the best of what we are as a country and as a people—survivors!—emerged. The city was rocked but responded with a will and determination. Law enforcement apprehended the perpetrators, brothers Dzhokhar Tsarnaev and Tamerlan Tsarnaev, in an amazing feat of teamwork, bravery, and skill. The consistent message from the president, to the governor, to the mayor, to each citizen, to every runner was the battle cry: "We will come back with an even stronger sense of will and determination."

That very next week I was in London for another conference and, coincidentally, it was the London Marathon with thirty-four thousand runners. There was a moment of silence, some new rules, and security practices. There was also one winner—and 33,999 victors.

Just one year later, at the 2014 Boston Marathon, we saw a city, a nation, and a world once terrorized now experiencing a paradox: a greater numbers of runners showed up following the tragedy, each fortified by adversity and now more resilient than ever. This group of runners is a powerful manifestation of the victorious spirit. Fearless, they are not deterred, as they start to run in Hopkinton and follow their will and determination to reach their goal at the finish line on Boylston Street. They have demonstrated to themselves and the world that they are survivors, that we are survivors, and that we will endure. It is our destiny! Go Boston Strong!

PART II

THE BIG FIVE

WE'VE NOW COMPLETED THE DISCOVERY PHASE of our journey. You've seen that we're all athletes, that victory is hardwired in our DNA, and that we can all achieve greatness when we capture the victorious spirit inside us—whether we're boosting our performance on the playing field or thriving in other areas of our lives.

On the next leg of our journey, we'll look at the ways you can feed your own victorious spirit. As I said in the introduction to this book, there is nothing to prevent you from attaining greatness, securing the awe of your peers, or shivering with pleasure from the mighty sensation of health. The forge burns within us, and in the heat of our passions, we will always come out magnificent and strong. To find that spirit within us, I have developed five key factors to incorporate into your daily life— the "Big Five," as I call them.

THE BIG FIVE

1. **Exercise and Nutrition:** By keeping to a daily fitness program, your body will stimulate endorphins or "feel-good hormones" that will naturally enhance your mood. But don't let a poor diet

ruin the strides you have made with exercise—diet and nutrition are just as important for sustaining a healthy lifestyle. When you're eating right and moving your body enough, you can perform well—and be victorious—at any age.

2. **Optimism and Hope:** Combined with exercise, positivity is just what you need to empower yourself to find and renew a victorious spirit. With a good attitude you can be mentally ready for any challenge, optimistic about the plan for success, and hopeful for a desired result.

3. **Adventure and Challenges:** Adventure and new challenges can create rich experiences that will allow you to enjoy unity with others, expansion of your cultural and personal barriers, and happiness in your current state. Even when it comes to difficult challenges, the insight you have gained through your various adventures will allow you to see that your goals are always within reach.

4. **Relationships and Mentoring:** Compassion and kindness are the highest forms of human emotion and expression. You foster the victorious spirit—in yourself and in others—when you show these to the people around you. There are many forms of relationships in your life: family, a major support system when you face adversity; mentors, who provide wisdom, experience, influence, and comfort when you don't know the answer; teammates, who you must work with in order to succeed; and even complete strangers, who you can share your compassion and kindness with while expecting nothing in return.

5. **Values and Character:** Character can make or break your victorious spirit, so hold yourself to strong values. Strong character and a possession of solid values are what enable you to be a team player. Once you build a strong character, it will work with your values and standards to keep you on the right path to achieving your goals.

In the next five chapters, we'll dive into each of these "Big Five" separately to see how you can find the flame within and unleash the victorious spirit.

CHAPTER 4

Life's Elixirs

Exercise and Nutrition

IT IS 5:00 A.M. ON A cold Monday in January. The alarm screams. Through the haze of sleep, I hear my wife's voice: "It's that time!"

I refuse to believe that the time has come. I hit the snooze button and just minutes later, the alarm squeals again as my heart begins to race in anticipation. This is a sentinel response, the signal that I am beginning my day. I whisper, "It's a great day to be alive." I repeat that out loud as my other self tries to convince me that sleep at this exact moment is more vital. In that one brief moment, I vacillate, with the brain and the mind in internal conflict, the heart racing and the bladder bursting. The hip twists, the knee flexes. I give a deep sigh, take a breath, and I get up from the bed. Yes!

One foot over the next, and I am ready to go. Well, I am almost ready, I realize as I look outside. It's raining. No, not just raining, it's pouring. Today will be a wet one. Downstairs I go, wake up the dogs, make the coffee, and collect the gear—the sweats, jacket, gloves, and hat. Once I step outside, the rain lets up a little and I only hear the natural sounds of morning: the hooting owls, the yelping coyote in the distance, and the beautiful morning quiet.

We start with a slow walk, then a jog, and we are off, down the road and up the small hill. "Boy, is it wet and cold," I think to myself as I dodge puddles and head toward the foot of the steep hill. It is harder and harder to breathe as I near the top. One voice between my ears screams out, "I can't do this!" The other voice supports my efforts: "You're only seconds from the top, almost there. Stay the course, no problem. *Citius, Altius, Fortius.* Faster, higher, stronger."

My face is wet with sweat and rain. My body is now hot with exhaustion and cold with chill. I can hardly breathe, but in a split second, a soothing inner voice responds, "I did it!" I reach the top of the hill. My heart is racing at its maximum rate. I can't breathe, but instantaneously, the endorphins kick in. I finally have awakened from my morning slumber. I now recognize that there is a world around me. It has stopped raining, as the rising morning sun breaks through an array of beautiful blue and pink clouds. I can smell the fresh scent of jasmine mixed with the cool mist. Overwhelmed with the moment, of the sunrise and the view from the crest of the hill, my arms go up. In this instant, I am at the top of the world. I have conquered the unconquerable. I am Rocky at the top of the steps of the Philadelphia Museum of Art, Harold Abrahams in *Chariots of Fire* achieving gold one more time, and Mike Eruzione scoring the winning goal in the "Miracle on Ice" Olympic hockey game. The music, the fanfare, the sights, the smells—it is all part of the intense experience of my very addicting and private daily run.

As a fifty-something sports medicine surgeon, I live a demanding and very Spartan life. It requires long hours, a fast pace, and hard, physically demanding work. This run is a daily routine, my way of getting in the zone for what lies ahead. Getting to the top of this hill is critical, and is inextricably linked to my daily functional success. It gives me the resilience and fortitude needed to achieve success in all aspects of my life, physically and emotionally. There are rare times when I feel weak and cannot complete the run. When that happens, I suffer the consequences of fatigue and feeling not myself. So I am an addict—addicted because I know that if I can do this on a daily basis, my body and mind allows me to function properly. There is no applause, no music, no crowd rooting me on, but I have learned that this run is critical for being victorious in my moment, my day, my life, and my journey.

As we grow through life, our health tends to escalate, bubble, and become strong, affording us all moments like this. But health will also quickly begin to decline if we do nothing to reverse this trend. Even the young can fall into poor health without attention to their physical bodies. We are biological beings, and the strength of our cells, organs, and systems gradually begins to diminish as we age. But there is a cure, so to speak, a pathway to maintaining health and discovering the heights that our spirit can take us if we let it have the reins.

A major premise of this book is that the victorious spirit resides inside your mind and inner self, no matter your age or bodily abilities. But regardless of victory as a holistic concept, the physical remains a crucial aspect of unleashing the victorious spirit. Will you ever compete in the Olympics? It's unlikely. You can, however, be a victor on your own terms by discovering that vigorous, thrilling exercise and nutritious foods are like the elixirs of life. I'm a big advocate of the principle that you are what you eat, drink, think, and do. When we escape the sea of processed foods and sedentary entertainments around us and choose better options, we bring ourselves more in line with that fantastic athletic heritage in each of us. And we give ourselves a strong foundation for finding the win within.

EXERCISE + VICTORIOUS SPIRIT = HEROICS

My morning ritual is just a small example of the steps that you can take to maintain your health, whether you're sixteen or sixty-six. Do you have a daily fitness program like I do? This will stimulate the brain neurotransmitters dopamine, serotonin, and others, which will enhance your mood. I'm not kidding! You may have heard of a "runner's high" caused by the mood-boosting endorphins (also known as "feel good hormones") that your brain naturally releases when you exert yourself. Jeremy Sibold, a professor from the University of Vermont, conducted a study to find out the exact benefits of exercise in regards to improvement in mood.[11]

For the study, Sibold randomly split forty-eight healthy men and women into two groups. One group rested and the other group was made active. The second group was asked to ride an exercise bike at moderate intensity for twenty minutes. Following the exercise or rest period, the subjects filled out a "Profile of Moods" questionnaire. They were told to fill out the questionnaires at intervals of one, two, four, eight, twelve, and twenty-four hours.

The study found that the people in the exercise group experienced a significant improvement in mood immediately after the exercise. Not only that, but their moods also improved at the two-, four-, eight-, and twelve-hour marks. The fact that a relatively small amount of exercise produced this benefit is probably the most important notion to learn from this study. For me, the main point is that participation in moderately intense exercise for twenty or thirty minutes, without killing yourself, can produce good feelings that course through your body and elevate your mood for an extended amount of time. That's a small investment of time that turns into durable mental health benefits.

However, Sibold's study showed that at the twenty-four-hour mark, the results for both groups were the same. What does this mean? It means that having an exercise routine *daily* is essential to maintaining your health and your mood. It's been well documented that even taking a twenty-minute walk each day can profoundly impact the human body's ability to thrive.

During and after exercise you will have a meditative, emotional, spiritual experience, allowing you the mental and spiritual clarity to focus on things that you are passionate about. This physical, spiritual, and emotional place has been described as being "in the zone." In reality, you have discovered the victorious spirit—our evolutionary heritage that is naturally embedded in each of us. It is there in all of us—I promise!

When you engage in exuberant activity, you can expect physical, psychological, emotional, and spiritual benefits every time—especially when you're doing it with fellow human beings. Just look at the Boston Marathon, the London Marathon, and other races, walks, and bike rides.

Attend any such event and you'll see exactly how exercise and the victorious spirit intertwine. It's always the same: human beings performing, experiencing, exercising, and feeling great! Individuals unlocking their win within through activity—and those collective wins coming together in a collective victorious spirit that transcends all the negative forces that come against us. There are energy, smiles, laughter. The excitement is palpable among all the participants, each one a victor. It's a relentless and addictively rich experience. And it's for everyone: no matter who you are, you put one foot in front of the other and keep going. It is a beautiful, reproducible, and contagious phenomenon!

Before we move on from exercise, an important note: mental activity—especially the kind that stimulates your passions—can also support the victorious spirit. Make time to challenge your brain, just as often as you challenge your body. The 2011 *World Alzheimer's Report* determined that cognitive-stimulating activities could even improve cognition in those who already had dementia.[12] So play music, cook, and participate in lively discussions to feel good and live better. When we put together the strength of spirit with the knowledge of how to keep our body and mind healthy through exercise, we can achieve greatness, we can inspire, and we can become heroes.

NUTRITION

Though I cannot stress enough how important exercise is, another necessity is diet and nutrition. The pursuit of food is no longer our primary goal in life, but making the best food choices provides us with sustenance to become victorious in our journeys. Ever since the days we were escaping predators and seeking prey, it's been about balancing energy in and energy out to optimize the performance of the human machine—in other words, striking the right equilibrium between the food we consume and the activity that keeps us strong.

It is easy to consume meat and dairy products multiple times per day and to snack on the processed foods that exist in ample quantities around us. With the comforts that surround us, it can be burdensome to buckle down and cook a meal, especially when we are accustomed to the three-minute wait—with no cleanup!—that a microwave promises.

But an important question arises: What is the cost to my health? It might be easy to pop a meal into the microwave and call it dinner, but what does this convenience cost our bodies? Diabetes, obesity, heart disease, cancer—no wonder health problems abound in our country. Even the youth in our country, equipped with high metabolisms, are becoming victims of easily accessible foods, and their health is paying the price.

Do you have a balanced diet? Or have you given in to the readiness of processed foods? Are you overweight? Underweight? Are you taking vitamins and supplements that are specifically relevant to you and your health?

Do you even know what your body needs? We all remember the "Food Guide Pyramid" from our elementary years. Although it has changed over the years, it still requires grains, vegetables, fruits, dairy, and proteins every day. To find out if you are eating the right foods, you can visit the website of the Center for Nutrition Policy and Promotion, an organization of the US Department of Agriculture, at www.choosemyplate.gov.

A comprehensive and dynamic nutritional and hydration program is important to prevent problems, optimize performance, and facilitate self-care when you are sick or injured. What that program looks like depends on your individual requirements and needs, which change on a daily, and even minute-by-minute, basis.

Our human ancestors created a system based on instinct, biological drive, and need. They could adapt to times of feast and times of famine. Life was driven by the hunt. They came to understand once the kill was made that the long walk back required them to drink the impala's blood for its heavy salt concentration; otherwise they'd become dehydrated. They survived by following rudimentary rules such as this, and they found balance based on the limits of what was available to them.

Today, it's harder to find balance. We see tempting foods at every turn, and we have a much deeper and more complex understanding of how nutrition affects health. For an elite athlete, optimal performance is predicated on the complex equation of three components: calories, fluids, and electrolytes. Preparation for a big event, race, or game in warm temperatures requires meticulous understanding of carbohydrate balance, glycogen loading of the liver, and intake of lots of fluids and electrolytes (not just water)—including during and after training and practice, and well before the event. The athlete's dietary program should be adapted based on the intensity of competition and the temperature and humidity of the environment in which they'll be performing.

The same principles are true for you and me. We must adapt our dietary program to our lifestyles, taking into account the types of exercise we do and the environment we do it in. Are you training for a marathon in ninety-degree weather? Or do you do light workouts three times a week indoors? There's a lot of variation between the nutrition and hydration required by those two different activity levels.

For most of us, just trying to stay fit with a healthy body weight, a maintained workout routine, and good eating habits is a challenge. It's beyond the scope of this book to make a tailored recommendation as to what you should be eating and drinking day in and day out. I can, however, tell you that it's always about balance and control. I can also tell you that, of all the nutritional markers to look at, the glycemic index is one of the most effective, especially if you're looking to lose weight or avoid gaining it.

Looking at a food's glycemic index helps us eat things that minimize secretion of the insulin that stores fat all over our bodies at all ages, especially as we get past age twenty-five. That's why it's almost always a good idea to avoid or minimize high-glycemic-index foods that have little nutritional value, many of which are "white foods": bread, potatoes, pasta, cookies, cake, and so on. These foods drive our insulin and our blood sugar levels up, thereby producing more fat. Focusing on this one detail will totally change your metabolism, shifting you to use free fatty acids in your body and mobilize rather than store fat. Try it, and even after just one week, you'll see a change in your energy, stamina, and your ability to control or even lose your extra weight. It is basic, reproducible, and it costs nothing but a moment of focus and discipline. This is what athletes do to perform optimally, and so can we.

Empower yourself with what you eat. You'll be able to feel it—that you are captain of your fate, master of your destiny.

RAY ALLEN:
THE POWER OF A GREAT PHYSICAL ROUTINE

One of the best examples of someone who very consciously leverages his hardwiring in diet, exercise, and passion for the sport is basketball player Ray Allen. Rumored to have somewhere between 3 and 5 percent body fat, Allen is one of the most diligent and passionate athletes of all time. He is a study in detail.

Sixteen years after being chosen as the fifth overall pick in the 1996 NBA draft, Allen has reached the age of thirty-seven, old by basketball standards. While he is one of the oldest players still on the court, he has formed a routine that allows him to continue to play at the super-competitive NBA level. Unlike younger players, who can jump out of bed and run onto the court, older players need to stretch, eat correctly, and practice well in advance of game time. Allen's regimented work ethic manifests all of these factors as a strict routine that borders on perfection.

The importance of routine and practice dawned on Allen at an early age. Most players believe that making the highlight reels, with dunks and handles, gives them a better chance at touching the basketball in game time. Allen, however, understood the most effective way to become essential to a team. "The one thing I learned when I was younger," Allen explains, "if your percentages are at such a great efficient level, then the coaches have to look at it and say, 'We've got to get this guy more touches, because he's highly effective out there and efficient when he has the ball and when he scores, so we've got to get him more touches.' So, that's under my control."[13]

If it's important and Allen can control it, then it goes into the routine. Every game day, Allen is at the court up to five hours before tip-off, while other players will get there anywhere from two hours to thirty minutes before the game. During this time, Allen takes hundreds of jump shots from different spots on the court. This gets his blood moving and awakens his muscles. Performing the same act over and over is why Allen has the most consistent and reliable shooting form in basketball. It is what made the thirty-seven-year-old arguably the best jump shooter in basketball history. His career percentage at the free-throw line is just under 90 percent and his three-point average lies right around 40 percent, unheard of for someone who has shot more than six thousand times in his professional career. Ray Allen leads the league in the most three-pointers made of all time. He is the last person that you would ever want to foul when you're ahead by one, and it is all thanks to his routine.

Allen's routine of physical improvement has helped him endure many crippling injuries, all of which happened to his ankles, and multiple surgeries. During his 2011–2012 career with the Boston Celtics, Allen suffered from excruciating pain caused by these recurring ankle issues. Further into the season and into the post-season, Allen's made-field-goal percentages hit career lows. Because Allen's form is almost exclusively muscle memory, the slightest hindrance to his routine can cause everything to fail. While this may be a negative effect, if he is healthy, it is a routine that can keep him in the league for years to come, regardless of his age.

Since ankle injuries are nothing new to Allen, he has developed a workout routine that allows him to focus on strengthening his limbs and ankles. This routine includes squats, lunges, and reaching exercises, all with an elastic band that provides resistance. Allen will also change certain elements of his workout in order to maintain his ability to adapt: one day he will train in basketball shoes and the next day in bare feet. During an exercise that requires Allen to catch a medicine ball, he will work out on just one foot in order to strengthen and condition his ankle so that it may function under pressure.[14]

Ankles are not the only things to worry about at Allen's age. All muscles can tense up or lock, so stretching to prevent this has become a vital part of Allen's workout and pre-game routine. It is even more important

when you're almost twice the age of some of the players you're competing with.

But even if his ankles are not hurt and his muscles are fully stretched,
Allen still has one more routine to follow: his diet. Following the right
diet is extremely important to him—so important that he married a
cook! Granted, he married Shannon Allen for other reasons, but Shannon is also a healthy eater who helps Allen eat the right food to stay
fit. Having moved to Boston with him, Shannon hosts her own Boston
cooking show where she, along with famous New England sports stars,
teaches viewers how to eat healthy. In her first year in Boston, Shannon asked the Boston Celtics' nutritionist questions concerning Allen's
BMI, weight, body fat, and diet, and developed a healthy diet for Allen
to follow.

And though Shannon is the cook and nutritionist of the family,
Allen has always been very strict and controlling of what he eats. "When
Ray and I started dating like twenty years ago," Shannon recalls, "I realized how important food was to his life, and that food was really a tool
for him."[15]

While eating healthy is important in general for Allen, it is essential
on game day. When it's game day for the Celtics, Allen eats blueberry
pancakes when he wakes up at 8:00 a.m. He then spends two hours
shooting around at the practice gym. At lunch, he eats a turkey sandwich on whole wheat bread, followed by a nap, after which he'll have
his favorite: chicken, rice, and asparagus. Then before the game at 7:00
p.m., he'll eat the Celtics special: a peanut butter and jelly sandwich.
(You might not think of blueberry pancakes and PB&Js as health food,
but Allen burns so much on the court that he needs the calories. Even
professional athletes need to match exactly what they burn with what
they take in. The same is true for us; we must always keep the balance of
the "in" and the "out" at all times.)

While there are many athletes who maintain their body through
workouts and proper diets, not many can perform or are as athletic
as Ray Allen. He takes the tools that other athletes use—diets, practice, stretches—and creates routines that his body naturally tunes in to.

Staying fit comes naturally to this ageless sharpshooter. He shows fans and fellow athletes that the effects of aging can be thwarted and that your prime does not have to be limited to a few years. Allen is an inspiration to all athletes by pushing the idea of retirement further back than anyone else.

And when his moment came, I was watching. It was game six of the 2013 NBA championship between Allen's team, the Miami Heat, and the San Antonio Spurs. The Spurs were five seconds from winning the championship, and Ray Allen, one month shy of his thirty-eighth birthday, scored the tying basket by shooting a three-point jump shot with five seconds left. It forced overtime and gave the team new energy. It was Ray Allen's basket, his poise, and confidence that reenergized the Heat and LeBron James. The Heat went on to win game seven and the 2013 NBA championship.

Because Allen took such care with his routines of exercise and nutrition, he found the win within—big time.

DARA TORRES: AGAINST THE TIDE OF AGING

In 1984, Dara Torres began her Olympic swimming career at the age of seventeen. Today, after three decades of accolades and medals, holding records and newborns, marrying, retiring, and divorcing, she's back in the pool competing at the elite level.

Torres first began swimming at seven years old in a local YMCA in Los Angeles, California. She effortlessly broke almost all of her high school's swimming records, all of which are still untouched today. Mark Schubert, coach of the Mission Viejo Nadadores and Olympic swimming instructor, recognized Torres's promise and brought her onto the Nadadores Team—the most successful swimming team in the US Nationals. Dara was then fourteen years old.

Three years later, Torres helped the US Olympic team win gold in the 4 x 100-meter relay. After moving to Florida and becoming a University of Florida Gator, Torres swam in countless conference meets, competing in nine different swimming styles and participating in twelve championship teams. In 1988, she was named the Southeastern Conference's "Athlete of the Year," during which time she had amassed twenty-eight All-American swimming honors, the maximum number possible. From the 1988 Summer Olympics in Seoul to the 1992 Summer Olympics in Barcelona, Torres earned three medals. She then retired for the first time, undertaking a career in acting, broadcasting, and modeling.

Before the seven years that she took off from swimming, she had competed in three Olympics, winning three gold medals. She had won countless national awards and the distinct honor of being the first woman to pose for the *Sports Illustrated* swimsuit issue. During her hiatus, Torres continued her success. She did very well as a model and created a very popular workout infomercial. Eventually, despite the success she was having, Torres decided it was time to return to her true passion. Many fans believed Torres's return to competition to be a sentimental notion, especially considering that she was thirty-two years old and attempting to qualify for the US Olympic swimming team after a seven-year retirement.

At training, her coach, after reviewing Torres's times, insisted that the timekeeper was screwing up. But he wasn't. Torres was back and faster than ever. At thirty-three years old, Torres once again made the US Women's Swim Team. At the 2000 Summer Olympics in Sydney, Torres added two gold and three bronze medals to her collection. She was the oldest member of the team and yet carried the most hardware of anyone. Not only did she win, but she actually broke the US record for the 50-meter freestyle, unprecedented for someone in her fourth Olympic appearance.

After her performance in Sydney, Torres retired again in order to focus on starting a family. Married in 2003, she then divorced in 2004. She gave birth to her daughter Tessa in 2006. Many were of the belief that even if seven years of retirement and turning thirty-three couldn't stop her, there was no possibility after giving birth that Torres could continue to swim at an Olympic level. But she thought otherwise and proved it.

Only three weeks after giving birth, Torres was back in the pool, training as hard as ever. At the 2007 US Nationals, she won the 100-meter freestyle, typically considered a "young person's race." Later in the meet, the forty-year-old mother broke the record for the 50-meter freestyle that she had set twenty-six years earlier, effectively stunning the swimming world.

She then competed in the 2008 Summer Olympics in Beijing, making her the first and only American swimmer to have competed in five Olympiads. Even more impressive was that these Olympiads were not consecutive, as she did not compete from 1996 to 2004. At the age of forty-one, she became the oldest swimmer to compete in Olympic history. These feats were all incidental to Torres. In Beijing, she brought her medal count up to twelve, winning three silvers and setting the 50-meter freestyle record for the ninth time.

When the Beijing Olympics closed, Torres spent the next sixteen months receiving and recovering from biotech on her knee in efforts to restore its cartilage through a procedure called autologous chondrocyte implantation by Dr. Tom Minas of Harvard. The sixty-thousand-dollar operation harvested cartilage cells from her knees, multiplied them to fifty million cells in a lab, and then reinserted them back into the knee so that they would reproduce the absent cartilage. Making it through the 2012 Olympic preliminaries, Torres moved onto the semifinal qualification round where she placed third.

To some, her persistence may seem absurd, but her ageless performance quiets these doubts. While the media preoccupies itself with the unbelievable breadth of her career, Torres remains realistic but simultaneously unconcerned with her age. She lives in the perpetual present, focusing simply on consistently performing to the absolute best of her abilities, not breaking records or shocking the community. While her three-decade career is astonishing in its duration alone, its consistency is that much more remarkable. She has proportionately crammed her active years with medals, awards, and records.

Sadly, having made it to the final qualifying heat for the US Women's Swim Team in 2012, Torres came in fourth by a hundredth of a second, eliminating her chances of joining the team on its way to London. While she admitted the loss was tough, in the same breath she noted that she was swimming against people half her age. The loss saddened many US swimming fans, one of whom was six-year-old Tessa, who wore a "Go Mom" T-shirt as she watched her mother compete.

Torres maintained her high level of success even as a single mother raising a six-year-old daughter. Diet played no small part in her ability to do so, either, as you'll find out if you read the books she's written, including *Gold Medal Fitness*. "Whether breakfast, lunch, dinner, or snacks, I incorporate low-glycemic carbs, healthy fats, and lean protein," she's said.[16] And of course she's also kept herself in peak condition through physical exercise, and she does it by progressing through goals, like we discussed in Chapter 2. When asked how she pushes herself to get in the pool day after day, she said "I'm a very goal-oriented person, so I set short-term goals and try to reach those goals. And when I have those days, I think about those goals, and it gets me motivated."[17]

The inspiration that Torres provides is not exclusive to mothers or the middle-aged. To anyone who believes doubt has any sway over passion, to anyone who thinks circumstance or aging holds any import over dedication, Torres stands as the golden standard of the opposite. She shows us that any dead fish can swim with the current, but it takes a truly alive one to swim against it.

NOLAN RYAN:
TWENTY-SEVEN YEARS OF HIGH-SPEED BASEBALL

Nolan Ryan is considered to be one of baseball's all-time greatest pitchers. He holds many pitching records by a wide margin and played more seasons than any pitcher in all of the sport. It is even recorded that during his last game as a professional pitcher, *after* he tore a ligament in his arm, he was still able to throw a final pitch recorded at ninety-eight miles per hour. Now that's heat!

Yet how does a forty-six-year-old man compete in a realm among players twenty years his junior, at their peak, brimming with strength and power? One might say experience, another might say tenacity—I'd say that Ryan was possessed by his own victorious spirit, and supported by a commitment to keeping his body in top shape. At forty-three years old, Ryan was a marvel. He was still blowing his fastballs by hitters at an age when most pitchers have long since retired—or have learned to depend on guile instead of power. But the Ryan express keeps chugging on, getting more unhittable, not less. *Nolan Ryan's Pitcher's Bible* tells us the secrets of Ryan's success, showing how the right combination of exercise, nutrition, and motivation can help a pitcher develop to his greatest potential. He urges pitchers to stay in top shape year-round, including specific exercise intervals to meet the individual strength demands of each pitcher's throwing motion, maximum velocity, and maximum weekly number of pitches. He also developed fitness programs for pitchers—including weight training, aerobic exercise, and diet—based on the latest scientific research and twenty-four years of his own experience as a major leaguer. Simply stated, Nolan Ryan, like Ray Allen and Dara Torres, outperforms all else over time because of meticulous detail and discipline in executing the paradigm that you are what you eat, what you drink, what you think, and what you do.

During his career, Ryan played for four different teams and had his number retired three times. Ryan began his stint with his final team when he was forty-one years old—to put that in perspective, most pitchers retire when they hit forty. He went on to pitch another five years, pitching two more no-hitters, amassing another heap of strikeouts and essentially pitching at the highest competitive level, even at his advanced age. A testament to his longevity comes from a young player who saw Ryan dominate when he was a child: "I saw him throw two no-hitters when I was a kid. Nearly twenty years later, he's getting me out."[18] Age may stop some, but for others it is their love, passion, and spirit, regardless of age, that launches them into the heights.

However, pitching for twenty-seven seasons with virtually no injuries is an incredible feat for a high-speed pitcher, and even more so for one at an advanced age. Maintaining the blistering speeds that Ryan was famous for was due to his efforts not only to use the proper mechanics but also to be open to criticism on his delivery, even when he had already been pitching for twenty-three years. "You have to be open minded," Ryan said. "Closed minds don't make progress." You can see from the facts that Ryan developed into one of the greatest pitchers of all time with one of the longest professional careers of any athlete.

The spirit, the energy, the pace, and the lifestyle—Ryan was submerged in the spirit of competition and in victory, and he took the steps necessary to ensure that he could pitch for as long as possible. Eventually his arm did give out under the pressure of full-time pitching in his forty-sixth year, but it blew out during a game, while he was pitching. His spirit roared, and he literally played the game until his body broke down. Ryan's dedication and valor create a powerful symbol of a man driven by the victorious spirit.

• • •

Whether reveling in the prime of youth or feeling the strain of advancing age, we can all benefit from the dual elixirs of life: wholesome, nutritious food and vigorous, stress-reducing exercise. The habits we develop in the best of times will be available to us in the worst of times. When we build regular activity and the right nutrition into our lives, we're creating physical conditions that help us unleash the victorious spirit and excel in the life of sport and sport of life.

CHAPTER 5

The Ramparts of Victory

Optimism and Hope

Ability is what you're capable of doing.
Motivation determines what you do.
Attitude determines how well you do it.
—Lou Holtz

MY STAFF, COWORKERS, AND FELLOW SURGEONS call me the "Energizer Bunny" because of the constant energy and good mood I maintain, even if I've just gotten off a fifteen-hour flight from China. Why do I put so much effort into staying positive, even when I don't necessarily feel like it? Because I've found that having an upbeat attitude is more motivating to my staff and team than any complaint about my lack of sleep could ever be. My attitude spreads to them, and everyone generally performs better and has a better outlook on the future. When we have optimism and when we have hope, we possess the two vital ramparts of the victorious spirit.

First, optimism: When adversity strikes, we absolutely must remain positive, viewing the setback as a motivator rather than a hindrance. In these moments, the victor harnesses his or her passion to see the misfortune not as a failure or a roadblock but as a marker of progression. This problem isn't the end of the journey, the victor thinks. It's just a bump in the road on the way. Of course optimism shouldn't negate our grasp on reality: realistic idealism is what we should strive for. It's vital to staving off the self-doubt that comes with unexpected hardship. It helps you see that just because something unanticipated went wrong along the way, it doesn't mean you can't overcome it and still reach your goal.

Optimism is vital precisely because, throughout the course of life, so many things *will* go wrong. Trivial or catastrophic, setbacks and upsets pepper our existence, but they have to. We wouldn't be human if we didn't run into problems. We wouldn't develop without the experience of them. Our lives aren't measured in a vacuum. We define ourselves— and are defined by others—by how we react to the things that happen to us. Every occurrence, good or bad, presents an opportunity for knowledge and growth. A negative experience doesn't warrant a negative reaction. We have to surpass our temptation to resent or withdraw from our afflictions if we are to learn from them.

Further, optimism, in its fullest and most useful form, is an action rather than a simple mindset. Our thoughts must not only be hopeful but must also be outwardly manifested in our actions and expressions in order to make a reality out of our imagination. We have to communicate our own hopes and positivity to those around us in order to actually change the reality of a situation instead of just tolerating it. With these elements of anticipation, endurance, recovery, and active communication in place, we can enjoy each positive moment to its fullest. Perhaps more importantly, with this understanding of the significance of an active optimism, we can make something out of any experience, even those that threaten our lives.

Combining an optimistic attitude with exercise and sport is the fiber that connects all the elements. It is always fun, except going up the hill. It is always an adventure, as there are endless trails, races, and personal bests. There is nothing that provides more hope and optimism than the elation, joy, and euphoria that you achieve at the completion of a workout.

Capturing full optimism requires that we move from anticipation, to endurance, to recovery and progression. Start by anticipating the resolution of the problem in realistic terms, both subjectively and objectively. *It is what it is. Deep breath. We can deal with this.* We can make the proper attitude changes. We can get mentally ready for the optimistic new plan and the steps needed for implementation. This provides lasting positive momentum for the next step—endurance—and for the recovery and progression that follow. This "optimism process" is how we prepare to discover and integrate the win within.

Hope is a close cousin of optimism, a force of inspiration that—if we let it—courses through all our lives. From the hopeful fan crossing his fingers in the stands to the players sitting in the dugout on a full count with the bases loaded, hope is an element that can inspire and uplift unlike anything else. It gives strength, forges purpose, and motivates spirits. But where does it come from, and how can we call upon the secret stores of this mighty ambrosia? The answer is simple—passion.

Think about it. How could you be passionless and hope for something? Hope is born from passion, desire, and longing. It comes to life when someone wants something so much that he or she can do no more—hope is the final bastion. "But what about fans?" you might ask. "What is it that encourages them to hope as they do and to feel so strongly about someone else's actions?" Ah, but here it is once again! It is the victorious spirit revealed! That is, the innate force that we learned about a few chapters ago, the spirit that courses through us all. It binds us in a great mystery, but a mystery that is surrounded by celebration and imbued with hope, passion, and excitement. It is the victorious spirit within that turns the fan into a player and allows him or her to share a common passion.

Though hope may seem like a passive force, sometimes it can defy all reason and foresight by beating the odds. But that's because hope stems from the great mystery, from the wellsprings of spirit and being that we draw from continually without ever even knowing how or why. Hope is born in the early dawn of a miracle, and hope wills every miracle into existence—indeed, no miracle ever happened without hope.

Let's now sit back and witness a few incredible stories of how hope and optimism can feed the victorious spirit and spur human beings to accomplish uncommon feats.

ERNEST SHACKLETON: ENDURING THE ICE

Explorer Ernest Shackleton understood the true value of attitude and optimism during the two years he spent trapped in Antarctica. At earth's underbelly, a frozen desert straddles black oceans and mountains of ice. The sound of its wind is interrupted only infrequently by the alien activity of humans. Brazen and bundled, few have undertaken the task of Antarctica's exploration, and even fewer have succeeded. Its ice, its storms, and its emptiness present a land of hostile and unforgiving indifference toward the living, a vast and uncomfortable reminder to us that we've yet to fully conquer and understand our own home planet.

By the turn of the twentieth century, the Industrial Revolution's effects had blossomed to the point where our technology had nearly caught up with our curiosity. Innovations in production, communication, and transportation shrank the globe and placed it in the palm of humankind, whose whims no longer seemed limited by technical ability. Global exploration became a primary setting for the employment of our advancements. We could now communicate faster, travel farther, and shed light on the dark areas of natural science.[19]

The target: Antarctica, the uncharted continent and the one place on earth that could still taunt man's intelligence with its daunting mysteries. Its conquest would not only be scientific but also generally symbolic of our entrance into a new era of understanding.

Thus, the "Heroic Age of Antarctic Exploration" was born, and the international race to the South Pole began. Through wind, ice, frostbite, and threat of death, expedition teams from all over the world strove to achieve the new "Farthest South" record, inching ever closer to the pole. Among the heroes of this era was Anglo-Irish explorer Ernest Shackleton, known today not only for his triumphs but also for his remarkable survival despite his setbacks.

Born in 1874, Shackleton developed a knack for adventure through avid reading in his youth. Stories of heroic pioneers and conquerors presented to Shackleton a world of limitless possibility for exploration. However, scholarship bored the young man, in spite of his intellect, and he sought out the real world adventure of his literary idols. With the turn of the century providing an array of novel technologies, Shackleton found his rightful place within the emerging community of Antarctic explorers.

Shackleton's first taste of icy adventure came with his participation in the Discovery Expedition of 1901–1903, led by the established explorer Captain Robert Falcon Scott. While the journey had its moments of triumph, including a new Farthest South latitude, it was riddled with problems. Food became tainted, sled dogs perished, and several men suffered from a combination of snow blindness, scurvy, and frostbite. Shackleton was among the afflicted, weakened and unable to uphold his share of the workload. At Scott's orders, and to Shackleton's dismay, he was sent home early to recover.

While Shackleton's experience on the Discovery Expedition was far from a total failure (he accompanied Scott on his journey toward the Pole), the voracious young man felt unfulfilled. He had only gotten a small glimpse of the world that he wished to surmount, and his early departure left his pride wounded. In the years that followed, Shackleton served as a trusted consultant and advisor for future expeditions and later found jobs in journalism, shareholding, and politics. As with his school days, Shackleton found his life in front of a desk unsatisfactory, and he eagerly awaited the chance to return to the frozen home that had rejected him years before.

Never attempting to conceal his true passion, Shackleton's insatiability attracted others, particularly former clients who eventually funded his endeavors. With the proper financial backing, Shackleton planned and executed the Nimrod Expedition of 1907. An utter success, the two-year voyage included an even farther "Farthest South" latitude and the charting of several previously untouched landmarks. Shackleton returned home a hero, receiving many honors and accolades, not the least of which was being knighted. His triumph boosted national morale in the United Kingdom as well as the hopes of his fellow Antarctic pioneers.

By 1912, Norwegian Roald Amundsen was known to have reached the South Pole. Shackleton had since filled his time with endless public appearances and some unsuccessful attempts in the business world. With the race to the Pole finished, Antarctica left few unaccomplished feats for future explorers, but this fact would not squelch Shackleton's penchant for expedition. One undertaking that remained to be completed, however, was a total continental crossing. This task had only been attempted once before and failed, while another planned crossing could not find the proper financial support and was abandoned.

Shackleton adopted the continental crossing as his own project and successfully utilized his celebrity to garner both public and private donations for his cause. With the proper funding, the trip was dubbed the "Imperial Trans-Antarctic Expedition." Shackleton planned for the expedition to be accomplished by two parties on two ships, one aboard the *Endurance* commanded by Shackleton and consisting of the transantarctic party, and another aboard the *Aurora* that would lay supplies on the opposite side of the continent and assist the *Endurance* party home.

The *Endurance* departed in December of 1914 and almost immediately encountered the turmoil that would characterize the entire journey. Within two days, the ship entered pack ice and was forced to stop and redirect, a process that would continue for two months. By February of 1915, the ice of the solid ocean took hold of the ship. Men were ordered outside with ice picks in an attempt to break the *Endurance* from the ice's grip, but the realization quickly dawned that the ship was at the Antarctic's whims. They would be stuck for the winter.

Shackleton ordered the abandonment of the ship's routine and modified the ship to serve as winter living quarters. "Dogloos" were carved out of the ice to house the sled dogs. Radio lines were set up in vain, as the ship's location was far too remote. Between February and September—seven months—Shackleton and his men drifted with the ice, aware that at any moment their ship could be pinched and crushed like a toothpick. All they could do was wait.

In late September, the squeeze came, the ship broke, and the water started flowing in. With plenty of time to spare before the ship completely sank (it took about a month), the crew gathered all they could—lifeboats, supplies, food—and retreated to the ice. With all previous expeditionary plans now aborted, and with the primary objective now survival, Shackleton planned for an on-foot march to a more maneuverable position. In October, the crew set out, carrying their lifeboats on sleds, hoping to reach a whaling outpost for supplies. Progress through the unforgiving terrain was sluggish, and the crew managed to travel only two miles in three days. On November 1, Shackleton, again having to modify his plans, abandoned the march. The crew settled on a literal island of ice drifting through the Antarctic, dubbed their temporary home "Ocean Camp," and hoped for it to bring them to a more reasonable position.

Again, they were at the whims of the ice, but the camp began moving in a counterproductive direction. In an attempt to reduce the distance that they would have to travel in a lifeboat, Shackleton ordered a second march in late December. Progress, while faster than the first march's attempt, was still slow, and the crew's morale low, again forcing Shackleton to halt and camp on the ice. A year had passed since the *Endurance* departed on its journey and, instead of being halfway through their triumphant trek across the continent, the crew was waiting for deliverance—at the hands of a drifting mass of ice, no less. Their new camp, the aptly named "Patience Camp," would be the crew's home for another three months.

During this time, food began running low, the sled dogs were shot and killed, and the chance of salvation grew fainter with each passing day. Shackleton and the crew knew their ice camp would eventually break, and so they knew a journey through the Antarctic Ocean aboard lifeboats would be in their future, if they lived until then.

April of 1916 brought the breaking of the ice, and the crew had no choice but to set out on their lifeboats to Deception Island, where they believed some supplies might await them. The island was properly named, as the crew was deceived by the island's attainability, having to fight off the rigorous tossing of the waves and constant soakings in ice water. Shackleton realized that reaching Deception Island would mean death for his crew, and so he redirected the lifeboats to the less convenient Elephant Island. After several days at sea, they were able to land on the remote and rarely visited island.

Now on a stationary land mass and still without external communication, the responsibility of the crew's salvation fell onto their own shoulders. Another lifeboat journey would have to be made for the distant (for a lifeboat) island of South Georgia, where civilization endured. A single lifeboat was customized for the perilous journey, to be led by Shackleton with five others, while the remaining crew waited on Elephant Island. Frank Wild, Shackleton's right-hand man, was put in command of the Elephant Island party and given orders to depart for Deception Island the following spring if Shackleton and his party didn't return. This was an uncomfortably likely scenario.

On April 24, 1916, the lifeboat, christened the *James Caird* after one of the expedition's benefactors, set out. The two-week, eight-hundred-mile voyage was accompanied by terrible storms, and the crew would later find a steamboat capsized. Land was eventually sighted and, after two days of fighting off winds that prevented porting, the ice-coated *James Caird* landed on South Georgia.

While people were known to inhabit South Georgia's whaling stations, the only civilization laid on the coast opposite the *James Caird*'s landing point. The only options were another life-or-death boat trip around the island or an unmapped land crossing on foot. The latter was decided to be the "better" option, and, after a few days of recuperation, Shackleton and two others set out while the other three remained with the *James Caird*.

The three trekkers climbed, slid, and marched through the island's unknown terrain for thirty-six hours straight, guessing their path the entire way. Tired and delirious, the men pushed on, unwilling to succumb to the ice after a year and a half of surviving it. In documenting the South Georgia crossing, Shackleton noted the unshakable sense of a fourth, ethereal presence among the three men.

On May 21, 1916, the three reached the opposite coast, and heard the whaling station's steam whistle. This was the first sound made by another human, other than that of his crew, that Shackleton had heard since December 1914. With external help now available, Shackleton first rescued the three men waiting on the southern coast of South Georgia, and he quickly began devising the rescue of those left on Elephant Island. Politics and economics made securing a rescue boat a time-consuming task. It took four boats, begged for by Shackleton from four different countries, before the Elephant Island crew was rescued, as the first three attempts were prevented from landing because of ice. Finally, on August 30, 1916, the members of the Elephant Island party were rescued, twenty-two months after the Imperial Trans-Antarctic Expedition's departure. Not a single crewman lost his life.

So, what was the spectral presence that accompanied Shackleton along his South Georgia crossing? He claims it was "Providence," an angel, a divine watcher, guider, and protector of men. But was it really a divine entity sent from the heavens, or could this supernatural guardian have come from within Shackleton himself? I'd like to think of this fourth traveler as the embodiment of Shackleton's optimism, without which the *Endurance* crew might not have survived.

Shackleton fully engaged himself in true optimism. In anticipating and planning his adventure, the explorer was notorious for his unconventional recruiting methods. While technical expertise was of course a prerequisite for membership, Shackleton was just as interested in the personal character of his crew. He inquired into his physicist's singing ability and chose a few men, after only brief questioning, simply because he liked the look of them. Shackleton knew in advance that an expedition of such grandeur would require a team that possessed not only procedural functionality but personal and emotional stability as well.

These measures fully paid off as, true to its name, the *Endurance* endured tribulations. In the lightless winter spent trapped in the pack ice, Shackleton kept morale high by encouraging weekend festivities and the celebrations of birthdays and holidays. Happiness was as practical as anything in terms of survival. He sent his men on moonlit walks on the ice to keep the depression of isolation at bay. After the ship sank, and when a food shortage became a legitimate worry, Shackleton scorned any sign of doubt in his men.

There were suggestions to stockpile seal meat; he wouldn't allow it. Such an action, to Shackleton, signified an acceptance of defeat, a self-fulfilling prophecy of death. Shackleton's optimism alone would not save the crew, so he relayed his hopeful motivation to them through his steadfast character. He was known to relinquish his own mittens and biscuits to his men in need, suffering the frostbite and hunger himself.

In the wake of the astonishing survival of the *Endurance* crew, I doubt anyone would have blamed Shackleton if he retired from exploration. He didn't, though, embodying the trait of optimistic recovery. In his dedicated persistence, by continuing to explore even after the trauma of the Imperial Trans-Antarctic Expedition, Shackleton was not just setting an example for himself, or for his crewmen. He was sending a message to the world, to anyone with ambitions, that no threat or obstacle should decelerate the might of optimism.

THE 2010 FIFA WORLD CUP: WINNING THROUGH OPTIMISM

A century later, the echoes of Ernest Shackleton's message reverberated off the walls of the 2010 FIFA World Cup stadium in Pretoria, South Africa. The setting was one of mystery and uncertainty. This was the first World Cup ever hosted in Africa. A terrorist attack on an African soccer team's bus had occurred only months earlier and, while it was deemed unrelated to the security of the World Cup, there was tension in the air. A workers' strike had taken place during the stadium's construction, and there was some political conflict regarding the "hiding" of slums from the tourist community. During qualifying matches, several controversies arose, involving questionable goals and crowd unruliness, building on the tense atmosphere. The neck hairs of everyone in the stadium, including my own, were constantly on end. We were all unsure if this tension would erupt or fizzle. This uncertainty only added to the overall anxiety.

The US Men's Soccer Team was in a particularly ambiguous position. While the team had improved since the previous years, the team was by no means favored to win. There were many sensational wins during the qualifying stages, most of which were counterbalanced with the disappointment of a loss. We qualified, though, and the players were set to face off against England in the first match of the first round. The two teams had not played each other in a World Cup since 1950. The match ended in a 1–1 tie, granting the team neither the inspiration of a victory nor the frustration and motivation of a loss.

Slovenia was the next opponent in line, a team we had never before faced. Again, the match ended in a tie, leaving the team only to wallow in the uncertainty of their standing. Any comfort in familiarity was far off, as the team was matched up with Algeria, another team we had never played. We, the doctors and coaches, prepared the players the best we could physically and technically, but how were they supposed to mentally prepare themselves? How were they supposed to anticipate an unknown team, especially after playing a series of such indeterminate matches leading up to it? There was no momentum of victory to feed off of, and no personal knowledge of the Algerian team to find solace in.

All that the team had to work with was their optimism. While optimism should play its role even when there is a certain momentum or level of comfort, it needed to be brought out tenfold in this scenario. We found ourselves more intimidated by the unknown, by the equal chance of glory and disappointment, than we would have been by facing a known soccer superpower. We didn't want to fantasize a triumphant win and make a potential sting of defeat that much harsher, but we also didn't want to sell ourselves short. If we went in pessimistic, our attitude would dictate the course of the match, and we'd be defeated before we even started. So, we had no choice but to hope, even if there were traces of self-deception in our optimism.

So we went into the match hopeful but vulnerable, floating in the disconcerting limbo of uncertainty. By halftime, we were no more certain of our fate than we were during the qualifying matches. The match was scoreless, and the stalemate dragged well into the second half. Both teams played hard, showcasing only their best performance to their unfamiliar opponent. Obviously, progression into further rounds was at stake, but so was the pride of both teams, particularly that of the US team who sought to solidify their compromised status with a decisive victory.

Relentless play continued into the eightieth minute, then into the ninetieth. No score. Would the match end in yet another tie, eliminating the US from the tournament? After all their preparation and dedication, would the team fade into insignificance without enough wins under their belt? For the US players, there was no time for these doubts in the heat of the action, no time for even the slightest anguish when each second required total focus and a fiercely positive outlook if they were to score. The burden of anxiety was entirely on the spectators, each of us holding our breath and gasping with every action. The Algerians played harder and harder as the clock counted its final minutes, but the US kept up. As the seconds kept ticking away, even those of us on the sidelines and in the stands could no longer afford to be doubtful. Our gasps turned to cheers. We each changed from a spectator of a potential disaster to a participant in the collective optimism pushing the team closer to victory.

In these moments, the only thing in the stadium keeping its composure is that steadily ticking clock. As the final minutes count down, a shot on the US goal is saved, and the ball is tossed down the field. With his world-class speed, American Landon Donovan sprints after it, ahead of an opponent by only a single stride. Advancing down the field, he passes. A shot is taken. Deflected! The ball lingers in front of the goal as an American and an Algerian tumble into the net after a struggle. Like lightning, Donovan comes from behind! The ball is just sitting there! The net is open! Donovan shoots! GOOOAAAL!

The US Men's Soccer Team won the game, 1–0, and preserved their integrity. While they weren't able to progress much further in the tournament (they were later eliminated by Ghana), the victory remains a key moment in last-minute soccer history. The team channeled Shackleton's spirit. In anticipating the Cup, the team maintained awareness of their less-than-best status but didn't let it psych them out. They needed to be realists to an extent, so they would be continually motivated to train and develop further, but they never took a defeatist standpoint. They never stockpiled seal meat. They maintained this stoicism throughout the match. In its final moments, instead of focusing on the ninety grueling, disheartening, scoreless minutes that they had already played, the team focused on the time that they still had.

The stories of the optimism of Landon Donovan, our best-ever American soccer player, don't end there. In the run-up to World Cup 2014 in Brazil, the dynamics between Donovan and the new head coach of the US National team, Jurgen Klinsmann, were not exactly smooth. Donovan asked for time off from the Galaxy and the national team for personal reasons, creating friction that crescendoed until he was unexpectedly cut from the roster just three weeks before the World Cup. All of the US soccer faithful, including aficionados, the media, and of course Donovan, were crushed. Rejection from any team qualifies as adversity, but this was his national team, his red, white, and blue, and his World Cup. This kind of cut really stings, and certainly can affect even a superstar's mojo.

Nevertheless, Donovan returned to the Galaxy immediately, with his game face on, to play against Philadelphia on May 25, 2014. Here, once again, we all witnessed his "ninety-first-minute optimism." Surrounded by his team and mentors, he prepared physically, mentally, and emotionally, and employed the Big 5. He was going to get up, suit up, and play on, no matter what. When the whistle blew, he was back to the process, the journey, and the game. The crowd was tense but came with signs and cheered Donovan on at every possible moment. Then with a burst of speed, the patented full-field sprint, the pass, the give-and-go to Robbie Keane, the sprint then . . . GOOOOOOOOOOOOAAAAALLLLLLL! He scored not one, but two historic goals and concurrently broke the all-time Major League Soccer record of 135! Optimistically optimistic Landon Donovan never lost focus but instead redirected his passion, positivism, and hope. As one door closed, he immediately opened another. It was so fluid and transparent for me to see once again, from the sideline and in full view of the world, that we were witnessing the victorious spirit and the win within. This is survival at its highest form of thriving!

We all have to do this in our lives, even during those moments when we aren't faced with a life-or-death situation in Antarctica, or a chance to win the World Cup, or break a scoring record. For us it is a rejection from a job or a team or a spouse, or that totally unexpected, out-of-the-blue injury or illness. From one moment to the next, we need to discover, incorporate, plan, and integrate. We have to look forward to the time that we have, to the things we can do, rather than to the things that we have done. This is not to say that we should ignore or forget our past, as we surely have to learn and grow from it, but simply that we cannot let ourselves get weighed down by the past. We have to treat our past experiences, good and bad, as fruitful in bringing us insight. With this positive retrospection, we can then look to the future, ready ourselves for what might happen, endure, and recover. With optimism, we captain our life's ship and sail the open seas of unimagined opportunity just in front of us.

MICHAEL J. FOX: AMBASSADOR FOR HOPE

I heard a story of a twenty-eight-year-old man who was on top of the world. He experienced tremendous success in his career and had even won awards for achievement in his craft. He had more money than he could ever imagine, and a wife who loved him. He was living the dream. One day though, his success came crashing down. He was diagnosed with a life-threatening degenerative disease. His picture-perfect world was altered in an instant by just a few words from his doctor's mouth telling him that he had Parkinson's disease. The man went into such despair that he tried to find comfort in alcohol, and serious thoughts of suicide crossed his mind more than once or twice every day.

One day while he was on the couch, drunk, his wife looked at him and asked, "Is this what you want? *This* is what you want to be?"[20] At that point, something in him started churning. She saw what he didn't— hope where there shouldn't be any. Ashamed with what he'd allowed himself to become, he made a decision to change. He committed himself to looking at his life differently and to anticipate the best possible outcome. His change in attitude transformed his life, this time for the better.

Michael J. Fox's change from feeling sorry for himself to living a hopeful life not only resulted in a happier life for himself but for others as well. "For everything this disease has taken, something of greater value has been given," Fox says.[21] The Michael J. Fox Foundation has raised over $170 million for Parkinson's research. People who join "Team Fox" raise funds through grassroots efforts, from flipping pancakes and selling lattes to running marathons. Even through all of his trials and heartache, Fox has let himself be hopeful. "Optimism keeps people healthy and helps heal those who are not," he believes.[22]

In *Adventures of an Incurable Optimist*, a documentary about optimism and its power, Fox asked a number of people how they would define optimism. One boy smiled and said, "Optimism is like Santa." He was right: optimism is a gift giver, one that keeps on giving. I have learned that optimism will help you and others find your way even when the path is not obvious. It is an attitude and a way of life that can and will drive us to where we need to be.

The one ingredient that is mandatory at every segment and transition is optimism. I have learned to control things that I can and to be better able to adapt to the things that I can't. I try to apply the spirit of the optimistic viewpoint to all things that come my way—both the good and the bad. This keeps me in the moment and has become the way for me to handle whatever hand I am dealt.

ERICA MANDELBAUM:
COMING BACK FROM HOPELESSNESS

Erica Mandelbaum, my sister-in-law, was a forty-year-old marathon runner when she developed Parkinson's disease. She suffered from tremors, loss of balance, muscle rigidity, and depression, which medicines and therapies did little to help. Then, Michael J. Fox and his optimistic foundation became the guiding light to change this seemingly hopeless, life-crushing situation. Inspired and motivated, Erica came to realize that there were new concepts and technologies that could help her.

This attitude propelled her to discover and intervene with a relatively new technology called "deep brain stimulation." This neurosurgical technique places a small electrode that stimulates the motor control portion of the brain affected by Parkinson's. Her response to this technology was so immediate and miraculous that she returned to running and was recently given a "Global Hero" award from the manufacturer, Medtronic Company. Erica, now a survivor and a thriver, has new hope and passion. She is poised to inspire, motivate, and help thousands of Parkinson's patients through fundraising to facilitate research and development.

We've all experienced loss—perhaps dealing with a goal that we could not achieve. The natural tendency is to feel that we have failed and that we are a failure. Then, the feelings of failure become the biggest obstacle we will face. These feelings become so powerful that we can be immobilized and incapacitated. We start to feel our hope slipping away. With these misgivings and the loss of hope, you lose your values and your core. The victorious spirit slips away, and you become much more prone to giving in to adversity and making poor decisions.

But we have to remember that we're all our own "MVP," that we all have an inner victor. The only goals that are impossible are the ones that we question. Stick to a plan and don't ever doubt it. Keep progressing, and always maintain the hope—like Erica did—that you can thrive in the future.

THE 2004 BOSTON RED SOX:
THE POWER OF A LITTLE HOPE

Some of the greatest miracles are born of the greatest animosities. The Boston Red Sox and the New York Yankees are synonymous with the word "rivalry." Their fans hate each other, their accents are distinctive, and their teams, especially in 2004, couldn't have been any more different. The Yankees were clean cut, sharp, and professional. The Red Sox, in 2004, were the self-proclaimed "idiots" who wore long hair and beards and likely didn't shower. The rivalry between the Yankees and the Red Sox is one of the greatest in sports history, and in the fall of 2004, a now-legendary sporting event occurred—nay, a sporting *miracle* occurred, all because of a little hope.

Outfielder Johnny Damon said of Aaron Boone's home run that catapulted them into the World Series, "We needed to get back here. This is where a lot of hearts were broken, and we're in a perfect seat to stop the hurting."[23]

Those were the thoughts at the start of game 4 of the 2004 American League Championship Series (ALCS) between the Boston Red Sox and the New York Yankees. The Yankees had swept the series thus far, punishing the Red Sox at every turn. In game 3, the Yankees beat the Sox 19–8, to which Bob Ryan wrote in the *Boston Globe*: "They are down, 3–0, after last night's 19–8 rout, and, in this sport, that is an official death sentence. Soon it will be over, and we will spend another dreary winter lamenting this and lamenting that."[24] Hope seemed to be dwindling, and even the fans were beginning to lose face and morale.

But did the Red Sox lose hope and become crushed under the stress of their losses? Did they bow down and say, "No one in the history of baseball has ever come back from a 3–0 deficit in the playoffs. I guess we're done then"? No. They didn't say that. You know what they did say? "Why not us?" They not only said it, but they wore it on their shirts in the games that followed.

Indeed, the Red Sox did not bow down before this seemingly impossible feat. What they did was harness the force of hope and imbued their bats, gloves, and spirits with it. They went into game 4, pushed the Yankees into extra innings, and won the game. They came back from losing in game 5 and won the game. Game 6? Again, they came back, won the game, and shocked the entire world with this mysterious momentum, this surge of morale, and everyone became infected, possessed—people were feeling that mysterious force within, the spirit of victory, sweep in from every angle. "Wait a second . . . Can they really do it? . . . Will they really do it? THEY MIGHT ACTUALLY DO IT!" Fans were ecstatic. Their hope had been momentarily crushed, they felt like all had been lost, but the team itself held on. They sustained their spirits, mastered their emotions, and brought every fan to new heights of happiness and excitement.

The 2004 Boston Red Sox took their fans, looked them in the eye, and said, "We can do this." And they did. Bars exploded in joy, shouts reigned in the streets, and pint after pint was drunk and spilled in honor of the victory. Indeed, the Red Sox came back for game 7, won, and sent a rally cry that shook the very corners of the sporting world. There wasn't a single baseball fan watching (except perhaps Cardinals and Yankees fans, at that point) who wasn't behind the Red Sox and mystified at their success, their unfaltering hope, and their incredible optimism. The Red Sox came back from a 3–0 deficit, brought about a miracle, and repeated with a smile, "Why not us?"

Curt Schilling was an important asset to the 2004 team. He was an all-star pitcher and a sure ace for the lineup. But before the American League Championship Series, he tore a tendon in his ankle, making pitching difficult and painful. Theo Epstein, the general manager of the Red Sox at the time, said that such an injury could easily put a pitcher on the disabled list for a whole season and that most players would question whether it was worth their career. But for Schilling, it was worth everything.

It was made clear to the Red Sox that Schilling would be unable to pitch in game 6 if they didn't do something to hold his ankle in place. Red Sox physician William Morgan found a way, and Schilling went on the field with three sutures and fifty-five stitches in his ankle. Schilling was already one of the best pitchers in baseball at the time, but even with his injury, he shined. His ankle began to bleed, leaking through his sock, and he bent down to scratch it frequently, but he pitched on, and the Yankees couldn't break him. By the end of the game, Schilling's sock was soaked in blood and he stated that he was completely exhausted. Schilling pitched one of the best games of his life with one of the most debilitating injuries a pitcher can have. But how? He had hope and the victorious spirit within.

•   •   •

Each one of us has the ability to manifest hope and optimism inside ourselves. We can calm our minds, motivate ourselves, and master our attitudes. But there are many things that we cannot prepare for, as we don't completely live within ourselves. There is an external, outside world that brings to us challenges and hardships that we must confront every day. Some we expect, some we do not, but there is always something that we can do to be ready: develop a consistent attitude of hope and optimism. These twin attitudes collaborate in a wonderful synergy that prepares you for any and all circumstances. Have hope, think positively, and the world will be yours!

CHAPTER 6

Creating Rich Experiences

Adventure and Challenges

AN ESSENTIAL PART OF THE JOURNEY to unlocking the victorious spirit is the ability to create rich experiences. What does that mean? I'm not talking about experiences that make you *financially* rich, of course. By rich experiences, I mean those times when you embrace an adventure or a challenge and come out on the other side a strengthened, more victorious person. I mean the times when you work to break down cultural and personal barriers, allowing yourself to enjoy unity, expansion, and happiness. I mean the times you step outside the daily concerns of your life and engage in activities that give your inner victor a chance to shine.

No matter what goals you have set out to achieve, making time for adventures and challenges along the way facilitates your progress and increases your momentum. These could be anything from skydiving or snowboarding, to visiting a far-off country, or taking a challenging class in a topic that you know little about. Sometimes you may feel like your goals are just out of reach, so creating these kinds of rich experience keeps your head up and reminds you that your goals are always within reach.

FIVE IRAQIS AND ONE AMERICAN TAKE A RIDE

The 2000 Summer Olympics in Sydney had welcomed the dawn of a new millennium with unrivaled aesthetic beauty and a collective sentiment of glorious renewal. In contrast, the 2004 Summer Olympics in Athens will be remembered for its aura of political anxiety.

The atmosphere at the 2004 Olympics was tense. Greece was hosting for the first time since the inaugural Games in 1896, and the century since had thrown the world into turmoil. It was the first games after 9/11. Yugoslavia had endured its bloody dissolution, and the nation of Serbia and Montenegro was participating for the first time under its new name. The ground conflict in Afghanistan was making the news every night. President Bush had declared war on Iraq and had already claimed US victory. US casualties approached a thousand, and the opposition had suffered nearly twenty times that. Thoughts and fears of terrorism were scarily real and at the back of everyone's minds. Although most of the athletes were not old enough to remember the 1972 Munich Massacre, I will never forget reporter Howard Cosell's anxious voice as the world watched the masked sniper cross the roof of the apartment where Black September, the Palestinian militant group, held the fated Israeli team hostage. No one wanted to see a repeat.

The Olympic community, as a team of nations, is faced with the painful contradiction between the desire to compete as international brethren sharing in the Olympic spirit and an acute awareness of global conflicts. Politics cannot be ignored, but neither can Olympic values be compromised.

As an Olympic medical officer, I was responsible for supervising the soccer tournament and addressing any and all the athletes' medical issues, from sprained ankles to serious injuries, to routine drug tests. Late one evening, I had stayed behind after many athletes and most of my colleagues had returned to their residential areas. Regular shuttles were in service, traveling throughout the Olympic Village and to the city's off-site venues where some of the events were held.

Australia and Iraq had just faced off against each other in their quarterfinal soccer match in Heraklion, a town on the isle of Crete. Iraq had won the match 1–0, placing the team only two games away from a potential medal, which would only be the country's second for any sport in Olympic history. The game's significance, though, greatly exceeded the sum of the goals scored. The political overtones were lost to no one. It was East versus West. The nationalistic passion coursing through the veins of the competitors and fans made the match seem like part of the war itself. The soccer ball might as well have been Iraqi sovereignty.

The shuttle pulled up and I hopped on. It was 1:00 a.m., and I was exhausted. I was faintly aware that there were other passengers on the bus, but in my weary state, I initially paid no attention to them. After a few minutes of being jostled along the hastily paved streets, I realized that the other passengers were five members of the Iraqi soccer team. They had been out celebrating their victory, and I was the only other person in the shuttle.

I grew anxious. Did they realize I was American? I couldn't remember if I had shouted a greeting to the driver when I jumped on the bus. Would they vent their bitterness in the midst of a random encounter with an anonymous American? Would they hassle me over the win? Over the war? Would they grow violent in their excitement?

I spoke not a word of their language but decided to listen anyway, just to try to identify any hostility in their tones. Yet they were so absorbed in celebrating their victory that they were barely even aware that I was on the bus. One of them was clearly the head of the group and, consequently, the most frequent speaker. I glanced in his direction to assess the expression on his face. He was nothing but smiles, and as I looked away, the whole bunch burst into laughter. They all high-fived each other, yelling something in unison.

The leader began to clap his hands to the rhythm of their chant. The chant almost immediately turned into a song. First one, then another, began to sing a simple folk melody that repeated after a couple bars or so. They clapped, stomped their feet, and laughed when one of them added a funny remark or shouted something extemporaneously.

Subconsciously, my left foot picked up the beat. I was smiling, having been infected with their elation. My previous worries were nothing but the results of exhaustion and paranoia. My head began to bob with the song and I realized that I had learned the tune. My eyes flashed across the aisle to the leader, and we mutually acknowledged each other for the first time. Without any hesitation, he lifted his hands in my direction and continued to clap the rhythm. I couldn't resist. I lifted my hands in response, started clapping, and began to sway the rest of my body. I joined in their song without even knowing what I was singing.

No language barrier could have obscured the connection that we shared in that festive instant. These guys were not my enemy. Our countries were at war, but we, six people on a bus, were not. We were just soccer fans and part of the soccer family. I didn't have to ignore politics, but I didn't have to compromise Olympic values either. They enjoyed the triumph of victory, and I got to partake in their joy, unifying us for that one, short shuttle ride. However fleeting the moment, we were together in the Olympic spirit, and we were happy together.

The theme "one team, one world" reverberated in my heart and mind. We didn't think about our countries' conflicts. Instead, we looked at each other as colleagues in that Olympic moment, as human beings. We were all the same. We were one.

As we sang, I looked at them with tears on my cheeks and thought about what it took for them to get to this place. This journey that they were on was filled with shock and awe bombings, hatred, disappointment, fear, and torture by Saddam Hussein's sons. Transportation, border controls, uniforms, training sites, and supplies had all been major obstacles in their path.

But now they had made it. They were living, breathing, and celebrating the Olympic dream. They were victors in their journey and, for being a part of it, I was a victor in mine. My time on that bus was the definition of a rich experience. Barriers were broken. Perceptions were challenged. And everyone came out of it energized and feeling victorious. This rich experience was one I'd simply fallen into, and that does happen in life. However, it is just as crucial that we proactively seek adventure and challenge in life.

NUR SURYANI MOHAMED TAIBI:
PREGNANT AND ARMED

Nur Suryani Mohamed Taibi is ranked forty-seventh in the world for professional rifle shooting. Taibi began shooting in 1997 and dreamed of competing in the Olympics ever since. She competed in the Asian Shooting Championships in January of 2012, where she made her dream a reality. Taibi, a devout Muslim who wears her hijab while competing, represented her home country, Malaysia, in the 2012 Summer Olympics in London, having qualified in both the 10 mm and 50 mm rifle competitions.

"Some people say that I am crazy. Some people say I'm too selfish. But I just ignore what others say. I just concentrate on what I want to do and what I dream of," she states.[25] The twenty-nine-year-old naval logistics officer is referring to the reactions that she gets from her family and friends when she tells them she will be traveling to London to compete in the Olympics. The reason for their reactions: she is eight months pregnant.

The future mother finds a competitive advantage in having a larger-than-normal belly. "Now I have balance at the front and the back," she says. "The stability is there."[26] Unfortunately, because she is carrying her future daughter, Dayana Widyan, she will be unable to compete in the 50 mm shooting event (where shooters are required to lay prone while shooting), although she qualified. She has been given the okay to participate in the 10 mm competition, where shooters stand up.

Even though many believe that a future mother this far into her pregnancy should not be traveling, let alone competing in the Olympics, Taibi remains resilient. "I am the mother. I know what I can do. I am a stubborn person."[27] The only thing that would deter her from competing is putting her child in any kind of risk. Before traveling to London, she noted, "My aim is to compete . . . if I have some problem that would jeopardize the baby inside me, I will reconsider whether I am going or not. But I feel I am strong and my husband says 'as long as you feel like that, energized to do that, it seems like that is your baby talking to you so you go.'"[28]

Joining her husband's support of her decision are her doctor and her shooting manager. Her doctor has told her that as long as she can stand the morning sickness, knows where the local hospitals are, and does not fly any later than she has to, she is good to go to London. Her shooting manager, Muzli Mustakimas, has gone on record saying that the pregnancy should not be a problem.

As far as Dayana goes, Taibi calms her every day before competing. She recites verses from the Koran, followed by pleas for an hour and fifteen minutes of "kick-free" shooting. Which usually does the trick! While she only had a few kicks to disrupt her shooting during competition, Taibi was not able to move forward to the final rounds of the Olympics. Yet she made her country proud, as the first female shooter from Malaysia at the Olympics.

Taibi is not the only woman to compete in the Olympics while pregnant, although she was the furthest along in her pregnancy in Olympic history. A Swedish figure skater in 1920 and a German skeleton racer in 2006 competed with their unborn babies in tow, at three months pregnant and nine weeks, respectively. Kristie Moore, an alternate on the 2010 Canadian curling team, had set the record at five months pregnant, which Taibi eclipsed in the 2012 Summer Olympics in London.

Taibi has created the richest experience for her despite all the challenges. Most people approach life with an "if only" attitude. *If only* I had more time, more money, *if only* it was the right time. Taibi rejected that excuse. She went for the rich experience. She declared her goal, focused, adapted, and made the most of the opportunity to participate in the Olympics.

FLOYD PATTERSON: A RICH OLYMPIC DETOUR

In the late 1940s, Floyd Patterson was a troubled kid sent to a special school for disturbed children because of his inability to communicate— he rarely spoke—and his frequent truancy, spending most of his days hiding in New York subway grates. He lived in a small apartment with his parents and ten brothers and sisters. His dad had difficulty finding work and his mother worked long hours as a domestic servant. One of his older brothers discovered boxing and began taking lessons at the neighborhood YMCA. Patterson's older brother showed promise and was taken under the wing of an amateur trainer. Patterson started hanging around the gym and soaking up as much knowledge as he could.

In 1949, Patterson showed up at a dilapidated gym on East 14th Street near his school in New York City, where he had been told that he could train for free. The gym belonged to an unknown boxing trainer, who in his unofficial capacity as a social worker, allowed the kids from the area to use the gym in the afternoons. Cus D'Amato began working with Patterson and he quickly realized that Patterson was a prodigy: one with a very undisciplined style. D'Amato was outside the mainstream of the boxing world and had developed a unique approach to prizefighting that was grounded on strong defense and moving from side to side so as not to get hit. The working partnership of these two men turned out to be magic.

Patterson swept through the ranks of the amateurs, won the Golden Gloves, and qualified for the 1952 Olympics in Helsinki. At first Patterson did not want to go to the Olympics. He wanted to turn professional immediately, because his family was desperate for income, and he was confident that he could make money in the ring. D'Amato assured him that he would turn pro as soon as he came back from the Olympics. It was a good thing, because going abroad for the most elite athletic event in the world turned out to be a deeply rich experience for Patterson.

The young boxer had never experienced anything like Finland. The boxing teams trained in a gym outside of the Olympic Village, which instantly put Patterson among the working-class locals. He was astounded to discover that racism was not a concept in the Nordic culture. He could sit in any seat he wanted to on the municipal buses, which was how the boxing team got to and from the training facility. The members of the boxing team became a very close-knit posse with no concern for race. Every day when the American team arrived at the local gym to train, they were mobbed by the locals and treated like rock stars.

Today, Olympic athletes are coached in diplomacy and etiquette in preparation for all types of international interactions. However, this was not the case in 1952, when seventeen-year-old middleweight Patterson won the gold medal. At the ceremony, he stood at the top of the podium, while "The Star Spangled Banner" played. A beautiful blonde, dressed in a traditional Finnish costume, handed him a bouquet of flowers then raised her arms in order to slip the medal over Floyd's head. Flashing his distinctive crinkled smile, he accepted the lovely bouquet and leaned down so that she could reach over his head to hang the medal around his neck. When she backed away, he slowly swung his left hand, holding the bouquet, behind his back, held his right arm across his waist, and gave her a courtly bow, as he had seen in the movies. Hundreds of photographers from around the world captured the moment on film. His glorious smile stopped the heartbeat of the world and shattered the stereotype of the "American Negro." Suddenly, the medal shining on his chest meant less to the people there—to the media, to the world—than the earnest gracious gesture with which he had accepted it. The innocence of his gratitude was heartbreakingly beautiful. This, combined with the impression of his youthful athletic prowess, made him an overnight celebrity.

When Patterson returned to the states, newly enriched by his time in Helsinki, D'Amato proved true to his word: Patterson turned professional almost immediately. He built up a very impressive record and bulked up to the heavyweight division. On November 30, 1956, Patterson became the youngest fighter to win the heavyweight title. He also became a father; his new baby girl was probably being weighed in at the same time that he was! So, instead of sticking around to celebrate, he drove all night from Chicago back to New York—understanding that fatherhood, too, is one of the richest experiences known to man.

•   •   •

As I see it, life is always a great journey—with many highs, regressions, and failures, but no destination. It's our task to find every opportunity for adventure and challenge along that grand journey.

I have lived my own life with a theme of creating rich experiences at every opportunity. It drives my present and my future. I am the ultimate experience junkie, if you will, professionally and personally. As a sports doctor and surgeon, I am always looking for new concepts, techniques, and technology; I am always in pursuit of learning and teaching. In medicine there is always a new challenge and always a way to improve. I'm also keen on adventure. For one, my career is punctuated every two years by working at an Olympics or a World Cup: new host city, new competitions, and new dramas. And my personal time is spent cycling, hiking, skiing, traveling, and diving, often in a new destination. There's always a new climb, a greater height, a deeper depth.

As an adolescent growing up near and in the ocean, I developed a strong love of marine biology, which drove me to work as an ocean life-guard for six summers. There my passion for all marine life—above and below the surface—coalesced. Whales, sharks, and dolphins directed my college major and a lifetime passion for observing, photograph-ing, and interacting with these wonders of nature. There's nothing that is more fun, rewarding, and exciting than to dive with sharks, whales, and any marine life. I have been to the greatest dive sites in False Bay in South Africa, Guadalupe Island, Fiji, and the Great Barrier Reef, diving—in and out of the cage—with the largest white sharks in the world. I have such appreciation for these animals and the grandeur of their interactions within the whole ecosystem. It is an awesome thing to see them swim and hunt, and just to have eye-to-eye contact with this apex predator. No matter what's going on, I'm always looking forward to my next rich experience—surfing the web for ideas and planning the trip. My passion for and pursuit of these experiences has become an essential part of my life—and a very enriching one.

Inspiring experiences like these are imperative to living the life that you want, so consider making them a priority. Finding, refining, and developing your passion for them adds all the color and dimensions that make life fun and exciting. Rich experiences can make you hap-pier than simply being rich. In order to achieve these kinds of magic moments, you first must work to transcend the preconceived notions and prejudices that might stand in the way of meaningful encounters. If I had given in to my initial fears and assumptions about the Iraqi soccer players, and not let myself be open to the joy that was happening around me, I would not have shared that inspiring moment of unity with them. Allow yourself to take risks. Stretch the boundaries of your comfort zone and embrace possibility—and all the uncertainties that go along with it.

There is an age-old English parable of the fox and the hedgehog. The hedgehog creates a geographical limitation and barrier for itself, as it is never willing to venture far from its den. Conversely, the fox takes the risk to explore his environment in order to discover the vast array of options for food. The fox is successful because his openness to explore his environment allows him to see and evaluate all the aspects that facilitate survival. We must use our instincts, courage, vision, and strength to overcome challenges that seem insurmountable.

All the individuals covered in this chapter created their own richness, reveling in adventure and challenge, taking risks, and refusing to be constrained by barriers constructed by others. Breaking down cultural and personal barriers is the fundamental key to creating rich experiences. By discovering the world around you, you will learn to appreciate what you do have, realize what you don't, and begin to makes strides to create a fulfilled life. The richness you create will last a lifetime and will bring you to a higher level in your personal relationships. Rich experiences allow you to feel a sense of oneness with those around you, which is essential to ultimately achieving success in your endeavors. With the backing of supporters to help you along the way, you will no doubt find the victorious spirit within and be successful in a rich life.

CHAPTER 7

The Jewels of Life

Relationships and Mentoring

If something comes to life in others because of you,
then you have made an approach to immortality.
—Dr. Norman Cousins,
former UCLA physician and philosopher

THINK OF THE LAST THREE PEOPLE with whom you've spoken. It can be anybody—a person on an elevator, a coworker, your spouse, anyone. Now write down the color of their eyes and the color of their hair. Can you do it? Do you know? Were you paying attention to them? If one of the people was your spouse, best friend, or significant other, I assume you can answer that question. But what about your coworker? What about the person on the elevator? Did you even talk to them? Or were you more interested in texting your friends or downloading a new app on your iPhone?

I bring this up because so often we look at people as stepping stones to what we want instead of as people with the potential to enrich our lives in ways that we could never even imagine. We look at the teller as an inconsequential necessity to getting our money from the bank.

We look at the waitress as the conduit to our meal. We look at our coworkers as people we must interact with in order to complete a job and further our careers. We look at people struggling throughout the world, whether in our own country or across the globe, and regard it as someone else's problem. For many of us, moments of compassion and kindness are rare in day-to-day life—even though these moments are the pinnacle of human emotion and can help us capture victory in both mundane and extraordinary circumstances.

A few years ago, I was in an elevator in a New York City hotel. It was a pretty big place with many floors and a huge, beautiful lobby. I got in the elevator on my floor and just as it was about to close, I saw a woman running to catch it. I quickly put my arm out to hold the door and the bright, chipper, and somewhat frazzled woman entered. She thanked me and we settled in for the ride to the lobby. My first instinct was to silently ride and entertain myself with counting the buttons silently to myself or watching the red light change as it counted down: 14, 13, 12. I resisted though and spoke up. "Glad you could make it," I joked. The woman, whose name is Dorrie, was happy I broke the silence and laughed. "Thanks, me too. I'm running late." I kept her talking, and through the course of our conversation, she explained that she was setting up a meeting in the conference room of the hotel and her intern hadn't shown up. I didn't have anywhere to be so I asked if she could use my help. She was stunned by my offer and grateful as well. So, I started a temporary job as this woman's intern, and what a decision that was.

I soon found out that this woman worked in PR and the meeting was with none other than former president Bill Clinton. I helped her set up a few things and sort some files; an hour later, with nothing but a few security people and a couple of aides, the man himself walked right into the lobby. I watched and admired the way he interacted with the people he was meeting. I saw him engage with a few other people in the lobby and then he chatted with me. He stopped and shook the hand of everyone in close proximity, including me. He looked me right in the eyes and said hello. He was charismatic, confident, and smiled a lot. He was instantly friends with everyone, and during our brief interaction I felt like we were old pals. It was an amazing moment for me, a once-in-a-lifetime kind of experience. And it never would have happened if I hadn't started a conversation with that woman in the elevator.

I learned a number of things from this experience. First, I learned that my interaction with everyone can mean something to someone at sometime. Everything and every one matters. Even if that woman didn't work with Bill Clinton, even if I hadn't gotten to experience that amazing moment, I still would have been a light on her otherwise dark and frustrating day by helping her. I realized that fears, even small ones like the fear of striking up a conversation with a stranger, can limit you and your life experiences immensely. Had I been reluctant to talk to this woman, I wouldn't have heard about her predicament, which sparked compassion in me.

From President Clinton, I learned the importance of how you interact with people, even strangers. He looked me in the eye for a number of seconds, he smiled genuinely, and he shook my hand. He took the time, the extra few seconds, to really see me as a person and to say hello. Now imagine a few years later, just after our game at the World Cup in 2010, former President Clinton visited with the team and me. We spoke about everything and he claimed to remember our first interaction. Don't underestimate the power of these simple gestures. Look people in the eye, smile, and take a moment to ask questions and learn about them. Make people feel special. Maybe it takes extra time to carry out one of these small gestures, but sacrifice that minute or those thirty seconds to do something that might impact someone's life. Say hello, learn their name, say their name out loud, and recognize them confidently. These are the cornerstones of successful human interaction. This is not epic advice, folks, but these are the things that will allow you to successfully create instant connections with people. It's these connections that are so important in building the strong relationships with others that you need to live a happy and healthy life, and to let your inner victor thrive.

YOU NEED PEOPLE

We crave companionship and will always choose to spend life with
another over being in isolation. We are social and spiritual beings who
thrive in packs. Social interactions and relationships are the fabric of
our human civilization. Biblical maxims, stories, and scriptures chronicle life struggles, dramas, tales, and parables. Yes, Abraham, Isaac, and
Joseph are the characters in the real comedy and tragedy of the human
drama called life.

In all of life—from our cells to our relationships—our biology
works relationally. In our interactions, biology varies in the forms of
symbiosis—two dissimilar organisms living side by side. In mutualism,
both organisms benefit; in parasitism, the host sustains life while being
harmed by the other. As opposed to commensalism where the organisms live side by side but have no impact, synergism (or mutualism)
exists when the whole is greater than the sum of its parts. Simply stated,
working together can benefit both more than working and living alone.

As humans, however, we are naturally selfish. We look out for ourselves and are the first to forget about the help—no matter how big or
small—that we get from others. I encourage you not to do this. Everyone, including you, needs others in order to succeed. Sure, you work
hard, you receive a promotion, you finally get that raise, and maybe you
start a successful company. That's great. But don't think you did it all
alone. No one can be successful by themselves. We *need* people. The fact
is, there are no self-made men or women. Understanding how to relate
to others should be on the top of your list of qualities to master.

In 1961, John F. Kennedy proclaimed his vision of reaching the moon
by the end of that decade. Successful implementation required teamwork on a massive scale—developing very collaborative relationships
between groups of scientists, engineers, lawmakers, and astronauts who
forged ahead to achieve the ultimate synergized vision, overseeing the
successes and failures of the Mercury, Gemini, and Apollo missions.

JFK famously said, "Ask not what your country can do for you, but
what you can do for your country"—a quote that reveals the spirit of

unity that makes us great. In the same regard, ask not what others can do for you; ask what you can do for others. Creating strong business and personal relationships is so important. It can't be said enough. When you put others above yourself, the group as a whole prospers, and you, well, you're the genius who knows the secret and revels in the success that it brings to your life.

Think about it: as you go about the business of living your life, are you more focused on "me" than "we"? The "me approach to life" is truly that of the hedgehog, focused on what is best for itself. This person operates on a simple formula: What can you do for me today? It is one dimensional, easy to understand, and simple to translate in everyday life terms. This is the friend that views your relationship not as *us*, but as me and whatever you can do for me. It's very difficult to establish close and detailed relationships with a "me person," because the conversation is never about us—the balance is always tipped toward them. With me people, the story is always about them at all times and at all costs. These are the individuals who never quite grew out of the self-centered mentality that we're born with, but that we hopefully age out of as we become socialized.

Then we have the "we people," the ultimate team members, the ones who understand and perfect the concept of the team. The richness of the team experience always outweighs the limited and shallow world of the me people. Whether in the workplace, in a family, or in a sports team, these concepts could not be more important to your success. Over time, any kind of leader must develop, build, and protect stable, compassionate, and trusting relationships. They should be your best and most prized possessions. Success is a team sport!

Remember the concept of TEAM: Together Everyone Achieves More. Teamwork in the office and in your personal life is essential. I have come to learn that the concept of "ubuntu," defined in Zulu terms, means, "I am what I am because of what we all are." It refers to the interconnectedness of all human beings and states that we are all part of a greater community. We cannot succeed without the help of others, and they cannot succeed without us. Translated: I am because you are.

Only together can we prosper. This is the essence of the concept of team. While rugged individualism certainly yields personal confidence and motivation, it would simply be ignorant, selfish, and insulting to those around us to believe that we are solely responsible for our own fortunes.

Ubuntu may be a local term, but it is a global concept. Aristotle, the ancient Greek founder of Western thought, famously stated that "man is a social animal," channeling the same idea of everyone's interdependence on one another. While it would be nice to think that our success is completely our own doing, we would at the same time be ignoring the myriad contributions of countless others.

Together Everyone Achieves More! Think as we, not as me, in all that you do. Remember others around you and create a core team with whom you experience life. Consult them, rely on them, and be available to them in return. Working together, the outcome will exceed your expectations.

THE MIRACLE ON ICE: TEAMWORK IN ACTION

"Eleven seconds, you've got ten seconds. The countdown going on right now! Morrow, up to Silk. Five seconds left in the game. Do you believe in miracles? YES!" So went sportscaster Al Michaels's famous commentary as the world watched one of the best-known moments in Olympic history.

It's 1979. The 1980 Winter Olympics in Lake Placid are just months away. Herb Brooks, coach of the US Men's Ice Hockey Team, has weeded out hundreds of potential players in the try-out phase. Twenty remain, and those twenty will go on to Lake Placid in February. Meanwhile, the Soviets have invaded Afghanistan, reawakening Cuban Missile Crisis–level tensions that had since subsided slightly. President Carter was going ahead with a US boycott of the 1980 Summer Olympics in Moscow. Politics, patriotism, and the Olympics were all so entwined and tightly strung that it seemed whoever won the hockey game would win the war.

The American coach had a challenge on his hands—his varsity lettermen were facing the Red Army. The US was still infected with a Cold

War mentality, and the perception was that the Soviets were ruthless, unscrupulous brutes who would be executed if they didn't win the gold, so no matter what, they were going to go home with a proper medal hanging from their thick necks. It would take a special kind of American team to compete with such an ice hockey powerhouse like the Soviet Union.

The Soviet Men's Ice Hockey Team dominated Olympic ice hockey from 1954 onward and had several medals under their belts. These men were well trained, and several of them had won the gold medal four years earlier. Each individual player on the Soviet team was impressive in his own right. The American players were talented individually, sure, but their hockey resumes paled in comparison with those of the Soviets. Even Brooks believed that his team wasn't "talented enough to win on talent alone."

But early in their practices together, "Team USA" barely seemed as such. Their old school rivalries were still ripe, culminating in fights, rifts, and a general sense of disconnected unfamiliarity with each other. In an early exhibition game, an embarrassing tie with the low-ranked Norway team infuriated Brooks to the point of forcing the players to skate sprints, long after the crowd filed out of the stands. You may remember the scene from the movie *Miracle* (2004), Captain Mike Eruzione exhaustedly yelling, "I play for the United States of America!" The Americans melded into a passionate unit of beaten-down and angry kids who, even if they couldn't win the Cold War themselves, at least wanted to prove their coach wrong.

The players' dignity meant more to them than a piece of metal; they had come too far for a disappointment. The US would have the home ice advantage come game time, but, while they were on an inspiring rise, the Soviets' steady domination made American optimism a gamble. Patriotism prevented total pessimism, but a somber realism had to be maintained to avoid the crush of the inevitable loss. Sure, they were not professionals by any stretch of the imagination, but the Americans had something that the Soviets didn't: strength in teamwork.

Brooks and his team began their assault on the Soviets by bringing them down from their legendary standing. Brooks knew that they had to "break down the Soviets to mortals."[29] A humanized Soviet team would be one that could be defeated. As long as the opponents retained their mythical status, the battle was over before it began.

One famous example of Brooks's humanization tactic was his attack on Soviet team captain, Boris Mikhailov. He insisted that Mikhailov bore a striking resemblance to comedian Stan Laurel. "You guys can beat Stan Laurel, can't you?" Brooks challenged his team. By taking even the most intimidating Soviets down to their level, Brooks was able to put his team into the right mindset to go for the Olympic gold.

Then it was time for Brooks and the boys to learn how they worked best together, and work together they did. Brooks also had an uncanny ability to recognize and work with talent other people found difficult. This is best represented by the famous "Coneheads," one of the team's offensive lines comprised of Minnesota boys Buzz Schneider, Mark Pavelich, and John Harrington. These three made for one unique "team within a team," due to their strange personalities and magical chemistry on the ice. They worked together so perfectly that their line always remained intact—no one else could play with them. The success of the Conehead line was evidence that three were better than one and that teamwork could turn a bunch of college kids into international hockey champions.

By the time the Olympics rolled around in February, Brooks had achieved the first of his goals: Team USA had become a family. Now it was time to work for Olympic gold, which they wouldn't have had a prayer of winning if it hadn't been for the relationships built by Brooks and his team. Before facing off against the Soviets in that famous match, Brooks gave his team encouragement in the form of one of sports history's most memorable speeches. "Tonight, we are the greatest hockey team in the world," says Brooks in the film. "And you were meant to be here tonight. This is your time." He knew that what the Americans had was special and that the team had what it took to make history. And they did just that.

The game began and, as with many of their previous games, the US fell behind early. In the first period, behind 1–0, they tied the Soviets, fell behind again, and scored a last-second goal, ending the period 2–2.

The Soviet's offense dominated the second period, with their characteristically high number of shots-on-goal, yet they only scored once, on a power play. The US, focused mainly on withstanding the Soviet attack, didn't score, and the period ended 3–2.

During a power play in the third period, the Americans jumped on a rare offensive opportunity and tied the game 3–3. Only a few minutes later, Eruzione scored on the accidentally screened Soviet goalie, giving the US a 4–3 lead, their first in the game. Ten minutes were left, and for the first time in twenty years, the Americans thought and believed that they might be able to beat the Soviets.

The longest ten minutes in US sports history began to count down, and not a set of American teeth was unclenched. The Soviets, realizing the threat of the situation, attacked, and attacked fiercely. These were the minutes that Team USA had trained months for, the minutes that Brooks had in mind when every belittlement left his lips, the minutes that required every ounce of physical and emotional endurance the Americans could scrounge. American victory became more and more possible with each passing moment, and when only seconds remained, victory was certain for Brooks's boys. All of their training paid off, and they left the ice as legends. As Dave Ogrean, executive director of USA Hockey, said, this was "the most transcending moment in the history of our sport in this country. For people who were born between 1945 and 1955, they know where they were when John Kennedy was shot, when man walked on the moon, and when the USA beat the Soviet Union in Lake Placid."[30]

The scrappy Americans proved the world wrong, but they weren't finished with their journey. The game against the Soviets was only a silver-medal round and, since Olympic hockey was round-robin at the time, they could have finished anywhere from first to fourth depending on the outcomes of the other games. Their underdog story without a final victory would ultimately be nothing more than a long-winded disappointment.

Brooks, well aware of this, maintained his patented I'm-not-here-to-be-your-friend attitude, assuring his boys that their win against the USSR was pure luck, in order to prevent any inhibitive cockiness.

Crucially, Brooks was a coach who understood how far strong relationships could carry a team. Sometimes the "best" and most seasoned players aren't necessarily the right players. And that's what Brooks got from his boys in 1980: the right players at the right time, the ones who were willing to play as a team. During the medal reception, the team lined up on the blue line for the playing of the national anthem, with Eruzione standing atop the podium. After the anthem, Eruzione had his teammates join him on the platform, intended for a single person. No image could more aptly capture the team's cohesion than that of the twenty men squeezed onto that little stage.

They had come together for the first time as rivals, children playing the game for themselves. They were all imperfect, and Brooks chose them for that reason. He sought out the puzzle pieces but left their assembly to the players. Through external conflict and intimidation, the Americans found motivation enough to overcome their internal, and comparatively petty, problems. Talent alone would have fallen short. Metaphorically speaking, Brooks found the edge and nimbleness of David over Goliath. A team of twenty captains would have self-destructed early on. They needed the leadership in Eruzione, the fight in Jack O'Callahan, and the calm in Jim Craig. The Soviets were a well-oiled system, a machine, but the Americans were a family. Standing in embrace atop the podium, they fully understood what Brooks taught them: the name on the front of the jersey is more important than the one on the back.

THE MANDELBAUM MANIFESTO

All I Really Need to Know I Learned in Kindergarten is a book of short essays by American minister and author Robert Fulghum. In his first essay, he explains how everything you need to know to be successful in life is what we are typically taught at an early age. Sharing, playing fair, being nice, and saying you're sorry are all basic courtesies that many of us forget along the way. Yet, Fulghum argues, these basic relationship principles are the only real essentials for living well.

I also made a similar list for my children, with the hope of providing a path out of the relational dysfunction that's inevitable in any family or team. Yes, this dysfunction is part of the normal flow of life, but it can stifle and choke the victorious spirit. Plus, I reasoned, how can I expect my children to know what to do unless I tell them? So I created a credo known in our home as the "Mandelbaum Manifesto." It includes the keys to understanding and navigating life in the simplest of ways, with the dominant theme being respect for the relationships that bind our family and community together:

THE MANDELBAUM MANIFESTO

1. In work and in personal life there is a balance between what we think we want, what we really want, and what we need.

2. Priorities in life are about the relative, not the absolute.

3. Listening is the essential cement to solidify any relationship.

4. Always tell the truth, never fib even if you may have done something wrong.

5. Always respect people who are less fortunate.

6. Do not fight over objects or material goods. It is never worth the time or energy.

7. Do not scream in the car when somebody is driving.

8. Never complain. No one ever wants to hear it!

9. Always have patience with people and things.

10. Timing *can* be everything. Wait for the best time.

11. Treat others the way that you want to be treated.

12. Do not talk or scream when someone is on the phone.

13. Always be polite, courteous, and respectful, especially in public.

14. Never use bad language in public.

15. Loyalty to family and friends is the most important asset that we have.

16. Never feel ashamed or upset by your mistakes.

17. Your reputation, your honor, and your word are like gold. Cherish them.

18. It is better to give than receive.

19. Never take the shortcut or cheat in any game at any time. It is never worth it.

20. You are only as good as your team.

These rules remind us that our ultimate relationships are with our family and friends. This is your team! Celebrate them, cherish them, and maintain them. Never compromise the integrity of those relationships for anything at any time. Remember that life is a journey with many stops, regressions, and failures. It is never a destination. Enjoy spending each moment with the people around you, no matter who they are. Spend your days reveling in the web of our existence and the collective victorious spirit that arises when we win together. That's the essence of *ubuntu*!

JESSE BILLAUER: THE MEANING OF COMPASSION

Of course, *ubuntu* shouldn't necessarily be a quid pro quo system. Our value to our fellow man isn't a monetary asset to be traded. Others shouldn't have to earn our compassion and assistance. While we do need to return the kindness others show us, we also have to be altruists. We have to help others purely for the sake of helping others, especially those who are disadvantaged and weak in some way. Moreover, if we wish to not only maintain the current level of social charity but improve it as well, we have to dole out even more compassion than we receive. And we all know that our world, however good it might be, could always be better.

In my years at UCLA, I had the good fortune to spend time with the legendary coach John Wooden while he was in his retirement. I spent many an afternoon in Pauley Pavilion listening to stories and vignettes that always culminated with a major life principle. Wooden became my teacher and mentor. I live my life with his teachings and principles as my guiding light. My annual dinners with "Coach" in his final years and our fellows and students are some of the highlights of my life. In these special moments, he would read poetry from his book *Inches and Miles* to the group and always left us with a quote. By the time of our last dinner, Wooden was in his nineties. His voice softening with age, he left us with his quote. "You can't live a perfect day without doing something for someone who will never be able to repay you." Those words are etched into my memory and are part of my personal mission and vision.

In 1996, seventeen-year-old surfer Jesse Billauer, one of my patients, was living the dream. When he wasn't in class at Malibu High School, Jesse was carving his name into the Pacific coastline with a professional career within his sight. Everything was working in his favor. His skill, his youth, his location, and the resurgence of surfing's popularity promised the youngster a future of fortune. He was on track to be the next Kelly Slater.

But on March 25, a wave pushed Jesse under, and in an instant, his fate made an about-face. He was surfing at his local spot, Zuma Beach, and the day was nothing if not ordinary. The California sun shined with its usual glamour, the ocean mist gave off the same salty scent, and the waves crashed in their typical rhythm. But the waves weren't the only thing that broke that day. As he rode one of the blue behemoths, Billauer pearled and was tossed off his board and swept under the surf. The force shoved Billauer headfirst into a shallow sandbar, and he felt himself go limp. Floating face down and helpless in the water, Billauer held his breath, waited for the next wave to roll him over, and screamed for his friends' help. A helicopter soon arrived. Ironically, only months earlier, in October of 1995, Billauer had been t-boned in his car. Waking up in the ER, his first words had been, "Don't let me be paralyzed! I'd rather be dead!" Luckily, the worst of his injuries were whiplash and a torn ligament in his thumb.

This time, Billauer woke up in the hospital to learn that the impact into the sandbar had snapped his neck and severed his spinal cord. With no sensation below mid-chest level and only very limited hand and arm mobility, Billauer was now a C7 quadriplegic. Initially, even Billauer's own father thought his poor son would have been better off dead.

Almost immediately, though, Billauer proved that he was far better off alive and paralyzed than he would have been dead and gone. After months of intensive rehab, and emotional and physical adjustment, he kept on living. He finished high school and went on to attend San Diego State University, where he studied communications. During this time, his friends, in connection with pro surfer Rob Machado and his sponsor, designed a customized longboard for Billauer, complete with arm straps to suit his predicament. Three dry years after his accident, Jesse was back in the water and happier than ever.

In 2001, Billauer joined forces with They Will Surf Again, an organization devoted to the development of adaptive surfing for the disabled. What used to be a small-scale family effort was now a renowned charity organization, dubbed "Life Rolls On" after one of Billauer's post-accident mantras. In 2002, the foundation was officially recognized by the Internal Revenue Service and was beginning to attract high-profile celebrity supporters.

Today, a decade after its foundation, Life Rolls On affects 100,000 people a year, raising spinal cord injury awareness and helping victims reclaim their lives. In 2010, Life Rolls On was designated a subsidiary of the Christopher and Dana Reeve Foundation, perhaps the most visible spinal cord injury–related charity in the world. They Will Surf Again has become its signature program, supplemented by an ever-growing list of others, such as They Will Skate Again and They Will Ski Again.

Jesse Billauer, still managing the foundation, also travels the world as a motivational speaker. His inspiration has led to several sponsorships by companies like Nike and Hurley, and Channel Island Surfboards even made a Jesse Billauer model surfboard.

"Tomorrow is never guaranteed," Billauer often says. We can understand this as a call to live our lives fully, to set personal goals and see them through, to let life's beauty triumph over its tragedy. But we have to read this message in a broader sense. Every day, whether we realize it or not, there are opportunities to improve others' lives, not just our own, and these opportunities are just as fleeting, if not more so, than our chances at self-improvement. Especially in such a modern, fast-paced environment, the window of opportunity for meaningful interaction is growing smaller and smaller.

Jesse Billauer's story is multifaceted and truly inspirational. After he suffered a devastating surfing injury that left him paralyzed as a quadriplegic, he turned his misfortune into a rich experience with his refusal to give up. Billauer is more than just an inspiration in his perseverance. He is also a true altruist.

To pay for Billauer's expensive medical treatments, the Billauer family held several fundraising golf tournaments in the late 1990s. By the time these expenses were no longer a concern for the family, their events were still drawing in publicity and charity, each surpassing the last. Instead of abandoning the still-growing project, Jesse simply redirected its focus, donating the raised funds to spinal cord injury research. He didn't need the money anymore, but he knew there were plenty of others in the world who did.

Jesse Billauer is a true altruist and embodiment of the *ubuntu* ethic. His community, his family, his friends, his doctors, and his fellow surfers all helped to give him new life, and Billauer's first step in the right direction was realizing that there was hope for him and others. He imagined what a paralyzed life could have been without the love and assistance of others, and he reciprocated this love simply by living, by rolling on. A preference for death would have been a rejection of compassion. But

Jesse Billauer didn't stop there. In his situation, it would have been easy to resort to bitterness and pessimism, to hate rather than tolerate his condition. He could've taken for granted the love of his family and the care of his community, believing it was due repayment for the price he paid for being quadriplegic.

But he didn't. Billauer knew that it was due to the generosity of others that he not only survived but also found happiness after his accident. They owed him nothing, but gave him everything. He reciprocated the compassion of others with a renewed passion for life, but this he did owe to them. To truly reciprocate their altruism, he had to exercise his own, helping those to whom he owed nothing.

This is the true moral of Jesse Billauer's story, besides the remarkable optimism and resilience that he showed in the face of catastrophe. There were paralyzed people in the world that Billauer could've lived his whole life without seeing or hearing from, but he knew that they were out there and that they were suffering the same situation he suffered. This knowledge alone was enough motivation for Billauer to reach out through Life Rolls On. His compassion changed his life, and the lives of countless others. His story has a beautiful beginning and end, as he will marry a truly beautiful woman, Sam, later this year.

"I don't owe them anything," we think, simply because we don't share an established relationship. They may be strangers, but they are people nonetheless. They are our evolutionary kin. So how about this: We are all born into debt, a social debt. We have been given life and the opportunities for a successful life that are in no way our own doing. So, turn it around. Take the initiative to set up the success of others, even if the favor is never returned. Your compassion can come in the form of Jesse Billauer's—bold and far-reaching—but it doesn't always have to be so. Take those daily, easily avoidable opportunities to reach out. Pay it forward, donate your time, resources, energy, and money to something or someone, and it will be meaningful. These acts of the heart can be small, subtle, even unnoticed; but know that you seized a chance to positively affect someone else. Find satisfaction not only in your personal happiness but also in the knowledge that you have done all you can to improve the lives of your community and the state of the world, at least a little bit. It will be the richest investment you have made yet. You will learn, and most importantly feel, that compassion and kindness are the highest form of human emotion, the form that comes with the highest dividends, taking you closer to the victorious spirit and your win within.

TERRY FOX: RUNNING FOR A BETTER WORLD

In order to be great, you need to perfect what others have already done. To be extraordinary, you need go above and beyond. It's not just about tying records, it's about breaking them. Extraordinary is exactly what Canadian native Terry Fox came to be, and in the process he brought together a nation. Diagnosed with osteosarcoma, a form of bone cancer, when he was only nineteen, there seemed to be a brick wall blocking Fox's potential. But as we have learned, it is in the face of adversity that our true character is revealed, and Fox certainly revealed his.

In an attempt to stop the cancer from spreading, Fox had his right leg amputated six inches above his knee. The likelihood of him being able to take part in any physical activities seemed an impossibility. Fox was in the business of surprises though, and he showed his incredible resilience a mere six weeks after his surgery. He did more than just stand up and walk, he actually partook in sport again by playing a round of golf. But this wasn't enough for Fox, and soon after he began to train for the Vancouver Marathon. His friends and family were skeptical, and many of Fox's early training days were full of slips and falls. No fall was ever truly strong enough to really knock Fox down, and on April 12, 1980, Terry Fox began his "marathon of hope" from St. John's, Newfoundland, to Victoria, British Columbia.

Fox did more than just train. He partnered with the Canadian Cancer Society to raise money during his historic run. Fox's ambition caught the eye of Four Seasons Hotel founder Isadore Sharp. Sharp pledged to donate two dollars for every mile Fox ran and urged his contemporaries to do the same. Suddenly large donations began to roll in, and celebrities started to celebrate the man who was doing the impossible and quickly turned to their checkbooks to support his cause. Fox became the little engine that could; yet he was still human and still suffering from a life-threatening disease.

By September, Fox was forced to bow out of his marathon after suffering from coughing fits and extreme chest pain. It had become agonizingly apparent that Fox's cancer had spread. He held a heartfelt press conference the day after he was forced to stop running. He painfully announced that his cancer had spread to his lungs; his marathon was over. By this time, Fox had raised over $1.6 million. His physical inability to continue the marathon was irrelevant at that point. Fox brought his country together. They were ready and willing to keep donating in order to save the man everyone had grown so familiar with over the past five months. Only a week after the run ended, Fox and the Canadian Cancer Society raised more money in five hours than they did during the entire run. A celebrity-filled telethon brought in revenues of over $10 million dollars during the broadcast. In April, only a year after Fox began his run, the foundation had raised $23 million. His goal was finally becoming a reality.

Among other accomplishments, in September of 1980 Fox was named the youngest person to ever receive the Order of Canada, the country's most prestigious award. Fox had not only become a national figure but a global one as well. As his health deteriorated during his final few months, Pope John Paul II sent a telegram stating that he and the world were praying for Fox's health. On June 28, 1981, with loved ones by his side, Fox lost his battle with cancer. Flags were lowered at half-staff around the country in honor of the resilient twenty-two-year-old.

Fox's goal was reached long ago, and it still stands today. The marathon that would become known as the Terry Fox Run, or Marathon of Hope, has helped raise over $553 million for cancer research. Prime Minister Trudeau addressed the Canadian House of Commons shortly after Fox's death, "It occurs very rarely in the life of a nation that the courageous spirit of one person unites all people in the celebration of his life and in the mourning of his death . . . We do not think of him as one who was defeated by misfortune but as one who inspired us with the example of the triumph of the human spirit over adversity."[31]

The Terry Fox Marathon and resulting $500 million for cancer research would not exist today without the inspiring perseverance of one young man and those who believed in him. Fox could not have predicted the immensity of the impact he was to have on his country, athleticism, and medical research. Like Jesse Billauer, he stands as a paragon of what it means to prize relationships and community, to unlock the victorious spirit through meaningful relationships and engagement with society, creating a better world for all of us.

THE SPECIAL OLYMPICS

Compassion and sport take no better stage than the Special Olympic movement, founded in 1968 by Eunice Kennedy Shriver to help create a world that isn't divided into the included and the excluded. The Special Olympics are a celebration of the abilities and accomplishments of people with intellectual disabilities, and it has formed a new global vision for the acceptance of a wide range of disabilities. The spirit created by these games is contagious to all who are involved: ear-to-ear grins and a palpable victorious spirit can be seen 24/7 on all athletes, staff, and volunteers. It is a testimonial to the fact that there's an athlete within all of us, no matter our level of intellectual or physical performance. In 2015, Los Angeles will host the next Special Olympics, the world's largest humanitarian event to unite the world through sports. I have been selected as the chief medical officer, helping to manage 7,500 athletes from 170 countries. The dedication, compassion, and *ubuntu* commitment of all stakeholders here will be unequaled.

MENTORING: TEAMWORK ACROSS GENERATIONS

As we know from this chapter so far, none of us can get along without relationships and teamwork. The individual win within means little if it doesn't emanate out into the community. One particular kind of relationship reveals this concept in miniature: the mentor relationship, in which a person passes along lessons and experience to another in order to uphold a system of collective, interdependent functionality.

We've all had guidance and support from mentors in our lives: coaches, teachers, coworkers, etc. On a more abstract, and easily ignored, level, there have been many figures, past and present, who have helped to give rise to our social context, our infrastructure, our economy, our democratic freedom, and so on. After even a brief analysis of this sort, we soon find that we are each a product of the world's entire history. We see the "butterfly effect" become apparent, where even the subtlest actions ripple across space and through time. Even negative actions can have beneficial echoes, either providing an example through contrast or contributing to a "greater good" scenario.

With this in mind, we cannot discount anybody or any action, even the past, the distant, the subtle, or the negative. It is almost more important to acknowledge these more obscure influences, so that we can better see how intertwined we are with the global web of life. We can then truly feel our oneness with the things around us and fully appreciate what used to seem insignificant. After we are able to acknowledge the miniscule influences in our lives, our appreciation of the major influences—our friends, family, and mentors—is multiplied many times over. We see that we would be nothing, or at least nothing of what we are now, without them.

We all owe it to others to assist in their fortune, just as others have assisted in ours. But mentoring shouldn't be viewed as a chore. It's a vastly enriching experience that can strengthen your victorious spirit, whether you're the mentor or the mentee.

ANGELO DUNDEE: MENTOR OF CHAMPIONS

What do Muhammad Ali, Sugar Ray Leonard, George Foreman, José Nápoles, and Jimmy Ellis all have in common? They are all world champions. And they all had Angelo Dundee as a mentor. As their trainer and professional partner, Dundee enabled them to achieve phenomenal success.

How is it possible that one man can forge champion after champion, as if any man he touched would grab a title? It was through his undeniable ability to connect and create a relationship that would strengthen them both. Dundee had a skill in keeping the fighter motivated with the perfect bits of speech. In just a few words, Dundee could take a fighter who had their spirit low and inject them with hope, adrenaline, and the thought of "Yeah, I can still win this!" Dundee never told his fighters what to do; he simply kept their minds and their spirits focused on the thoughts of victory.[32]

Dundee was not a fighter and never aspired to be. He got his start through his brother Chris, who was having some success as a promoter. One afternoon, Dundee was in Lexington, Kentucky, with his fighter Willie Pastrano, sitting in their hotel room taking it easy. The phone rang. A precocious kid in the lobby wanted to come up to discuss training. Dundee and Pastrano agreed only because they had nothing better to do.

A few minutes later, a fifteen-year-old kid named Cassius Clay and his younger brother Rudy were sitting in the crowded hotel room, firing questions a mile a minute. From that day on, every time Dundee and Pastrano were in Louisville, Clay was pestering them in the gym. One day, Clay persuaded Dundee to let him spar a few rounds with Pastrano. After two rounds, Dundee had to stop the spar and get Clay out of the ring. Clay was clobbering the professional—and he was only sixteen.

Before long, Clay went on to win the gold medal in his weight class at the PanAm Games and then again at the 1960 Summer Olympics in Rome. He returned to Louisville and was taken under the wing of a group of wealthy Louisville businessmen. When it came time turn professional and choose a trainer, Clay said he only wanted to work with Angelo. The deal was made and Cassius moved to Miami where Dundee and his brother had set up the Fifth Street Gym. Clay never worked with another trainer his entire professional career. He had other players on the team who made significant contributions to his success, but Dundee was the common denominator throughout Clay's career and the single most influential partner in his professional life.

"I never touched that natural stuff with him," Dundee recalled in his memoir, *My View From the Corner*. "So every now and then I'd subtly suggest some move or other to him, couching it as if it were something he was already doing. I'd say something like: 'You're getting that jab down real good. You're bending your knees now and you're putting a lot of snap into it.' Now, he had never thrown a jab, but it was a way of letting him think it was his idea, his innovation."[33]

When Cassius Clay became Muhammad Ali, Dundee stood by him in the controversy of the Nation of Islam, the only white member of his inner circle. When an irritating liniment found its way from Sonny Liston's gloves to Ali's eyes, Dundee worked furiously with a sponge and water for the single minute he had between rounds. When the bell rang for Round 5, Ali was still blind from the irritant and wanted to throw in the towel. Dundee literally pushed him off the stool and back into the ring. Less than ten minutes later, Ali was the heavyweight champion of the world. When Ali refused to go to Vietnam and was stripped of the heavyweight championship, Dundee never gave up on his protégé and continued to work with him when Ali was in Miami. When Ali's hands were so broken and shattered that Dr. Pacheco had to shoot them full of Novocain to deaden the pain, Dundee carefully wrapped those precious hands before tying Ali into the gloves. In 2011, a frail Ali sent a video greeting to Dundee's ninetieth birthday party. Several months later, Dundee flew to Louisville to attend Ali's seventieth birthday party. A few weeks after that, Ali attended Dundee's funeral.

Both of these men would have been great had they never met each other. But working as a team, they became unstoppable. Who can quantify the value of Angelo Dundee's contribution to the myth of Muhammad Ali? The truth is in the fact that the partnership was never broken off by either party and the relationship endured despite the most dramatic career of anyone who has ever held the heavyweight title.

MUTUAL MENTORSHIP: BILL AND TOM

"There is an old saying about the strength of the wolf is the pack," Bill Belichick explained. "I think there is a lot of truth to that."[34] His relationship with Tom Brady shows the strength of that truth—when combined, they became more than the sum of their parts, an unbeatable team. But they also showed that mentoring doesn't have to happen like we usually imagine: with an older person mentoring a younger, less experienced person. Instead, if we open ourselves to the possibility, we can mentor and be mentored by almost anyone in our lives who has wisdom to give, no matter their age or station.

In 2000, when the now-famous duo first met, New England Patriots quarterback Tom Brady and head coach Bill Belichick were lone wolves. The sleek and smiling Brady hardly seemed compatible with the drab, ever-scowling Belichick. But their startling difference went much deeper than their comically contrasting appearances, lending much doubt to fans at the onset of their relationship. Brady was a youthful, energetic, promising-but-amateur offensive player; Belichick a subdued, veteran, defensive expert. Brady was an eager optimist, Belichick a seasoned stoic. It was youth versus age, innocence versus experience, and hope versus reserve. The pairing was anything but promising.

Then how does the Brady-Belichick pair continue to thrive today, after over a decade of football together? Moreover, how did the duo bring the Patriots the most regular-season wins (124) and Super Bowl appearances (five, with three wins) of any quarterback-coach pair in the history of the NFL? There was already Noll and Bradshaw, Levy and Kelly, and Shula and Marino, all legends of the game. But now there is Belichick and Brady, and everyone falls under their shadow.

No one would have anticipated such a success when Brady, the then-unknown youth, was chosen by the Pats in the lowly sixth round of the 2000 draft. He sat his first season as the team's fourth-string quarterback. Most NFL teams didn't even have that many quarterbacks. By the end of the 2000 season, Brady had moved his way up to the second-string seat but still warmed the bench while star quarterback Drew Bledsoe led the team.

Early in the 2001 season, serendipity played its role when Bledsoe suffered the injury that would eventually end his career with the Patriots. In that dire moment, Belichick put in Brady, and New England held their breath and watched. Could he hold up as a pro? What would the team do without the tried and true Bledsoe? Brady's performance, while adequate, was less than stellar, and the Pats lost the game. In the course of the next few games, he seemed to find his footing, and the team progressed their way to the playoffs, then through the playoffs. They eventually won the Super Bowl that year, but Brady was still far from the all-star status that he enjoys today. Beginner's luck, everyone thought. At the time, the newbie was playing a mere supporting role in the powerhouse team, a collective offense and defense that seemed unstoppable no matter what schmo snapped the ball.

As the seasons progressed, however, the Pats' defensive lineup dwindled, and more and more weight was put on Brady's shoulders. Belichick already understood the importance of personalized coaching. He came from a special team's background and knew that each player required a different style and amount of coaching to fulfill their purpose. But this technique would have to be elevated to an entirely new level when the success of the team depended greatly on Brady alone. Brady and Belichick's relationship began to mimic many romantic relationship patterns. They had already gone on their honeymoon, each enthralled with the novel relationship. Belichick had come from a mediocre coaching career with the Browns, Brady was fresh out of the University of Michigan, and the two had just won their first Super Bowl. Nothing could be better.

As time passed, however, their infatuation wore off, and the power struggle began. Who's more important: the player completing the passes or the man calling the plays? The tension only grew with the more one-on-one time they spent together, but there was no room for quarreling. Their relationship was the most crucial one in the team. Brady, newly confident and high off of his out-of-the-gate success, could have easily clashed with Belichick, rigid in his experience, and vice versa. But in a game where the quarterback-coach relationship is so vital to the success of the entire team, the concept of *ubuntu* quickly came face-to-face with their craving for personal gratification. Both men knew that opposition would be futile, destructive, and eventually end in their "divorce." Their relationship would either have to endure or end immediately, as any hesitation or prolonged conflict would threaten to tank the entire franchise.

Rather than giving in to their pride, Brady and Belichick instead opted to adapt to one another's distinctive styles for the sake of the team, eventually maturing to a stage of mutual respect and understanding. In any relationship—professional, social, romantic—the member parties are faced with an inevitable choice: to polarize or to magnetize. Any two people, no matter how compatible, will be different in one way or another. Once these incompatibilities are recognized, the health of the relationship depends on this choice. Brady and Belichick were no exception.

In such a make-it-or-break-it scenario, do you choose to oppose the dissimilarities of the other or to embrace them? It is entirely a matter of perspective. Do you take offense at the difference or embrace the diversity? Brady and Belichick chose the latter, which, several Super Bowl rings later, would prove to be the right choice for the team. Neither of the two would or could compromise their defining characteristics; this was certain. The only option, next to failure, was acceptance. Brady grew to understand Belichick's expertise, despite his sometimes-cold façade. Belichick grew to embrace Brady's skill, despite his novelty. Incrementally, the two found a mutual system wherein each could exercise his best qualities without having to conflict with the other's.

In time, they were finishing each other's sentences. The seamlessness of their cooperation seemed almost telepathic. Not only were they the most fearsome quarterback-coach team the league had seen in years, but both Brady and Belichick seemed to transform as individuals through their relationship as well. Belichick infused a newfound energy and experimentation into his militaristic strategy. Brady's mentality and drive became as focused as his laser cannon arm.

In retrospect, Brady and Belichick seem far more than just two people who happened to gel with each other. It seems that, before their relationship, they were two lingering halves of a complete entity and only fully actualized themselves in their unity. After they grew to understand, embrace, and feed off of each other, nothing could stop them. They were locked in place together. Not even 2007's "Spygate," when the Patriots were accused of filming their opponents' sideline calls, threatened their unity. As a result of the scandal, Belichick was handed the biggest fine the league has ever seen, and the team was horribly stigmatized. How did Brady and Belichick bounce back? They played an undefeated regular season, earning Belichick the 2007 NFL Coach of the Year award, that's how. Five years later, the two continue to make up the still-winning Patriots' backbone and show no signs of buckling under the pressure of tests to come.

Through the example of Brady and Belichick, we see that mentorship is much more multiform than we may think, not always adhering to the typical teacher-student, authority-subordinate model. Both men were simultaneously teaching and learning, back and forth. The two men's drastic dissimilarity, initially an obstacle, later proved to be the core of their successful relationship. They are the epitome of the yin-yang concept, and we can all learn from them that the key to a mutually productive relationship is not similarity or likeability, but respect and understanding. We have to be open to our mentors, as well as to those who we are also mentoring. We have to give everyone we encounter the benefit of the doubt, tossing away any vanity, because they more than likely have something to teach us, and we always have something more to learn.

• • •

As we set out to find our win within, it's vital that we learn to cultivate our relationships with the people around us, whether it's with a team, with the community at large, or with a mentor—and whether it's on the micro scale or the macro. Discovering and integrating your compassion for others, and the interrelationships that bind all of us together, will impact others as it illuminates the path in front you. Success is always based on the sum of all of your relationships in evolution over time. That is the equity and the real value proposition. On the other hand, losing sight of our interdependence is a surefire way to weaken the victorious spirit. As you celebrate unity and cooperation and compassion, putting the we before the me, your victorious spirit grows, enveloping you and everyone around you: just another way to find out that the win is within.

CHAPTER 8

Fair Play

Values and Standards to Live By

Your reputation, word, and honor are
the most important possessions you own.
—Abraham Lincoln

CHARACTER COUNTS. EVERYTHING YOU SAY AND do matters to someone at some time, so always try to do the right thing. There's an old saying, that your true character is revealed when no one else is looking. Clive Charles would preach, "Do the right thing 100 percent of the time." Strong character and a possession of core values are what enable you to be a team player. Fair play is the centerpiece of any team, program, or business model. Sometimes character can make or break your victorious spirit. Those who possess a foundation of core values and strong character often triumph in the face of adversity, while others who become intoxicated by fame or fortune can lose sight of the victorious spirit within and endure a tragic fall from grace.

There are no exceptions when it comes to character. Michael Josephson, president of the Josephson Institute, a nonprofit organization dedicated to improving the ethical quality of society, understands just how much character counts. The Josephson Institute breaks character down into six individual pillars that are essential to building strong character: trustworthiness, respect, responsibility, fairness, caring, and citizenship.[35] These six ethical values are the very components of character. Character is just one element of the victorious spirit. Once you are able to build up your character, it will work with your values and standards to keep you on the right path to achieving your goals.

John Wooden, who coached the basketball team at UCLA for twenty-seven years, is known for his stellar record and his inspiring example of principles in action. Under his direction, the Bruins won 620 games and lost only 147. They won ten NCAA championships and went undefeated through four different complete seasons. Wooden's Bruins established a still-standing record of an eighty-eight-game winning streak before losing on January 19, 1974, to Notre Dame, 71–70. How did they do it? Wooden always said, "Success is peace of mind, which is a direct result of self-satisfaction in knowing you did your best to become the best you are capable of becoming."[36] And when he says "the best," he doesn't mean just physically; he means your character, too.

When looking at Wooden's wide body of written work about leadership, coaching, and success, we see this clearly. He developed a simple system of values that, when enacted, will strengthen character and lead people to becoming the best they can be. In his book, *Wooden: A Lifetime of Observations and Reflections On and Off the Court*, Wooden reveals his "Nine Promises That Can Bring Happiness," which include several that focus on character, such as:

- Promise to think only of the best, to work only for the best, and to expect only the best in yourself and others.

- Promise to be just as enthusiastic about the success of others as you are about your own.

- Promise to give so much time improving yourself that you have no time to criticize others.

These easy-to-remember mantras are fantastic for keeping yourself on track in the character department. And Wooden has plenty of them. Later in the same book, he expands upon the Nine Promises with his "Eight Suggestions for Succeeding," which are even more explicit about the importance of character:

- Fear no opponent. Respect every opponent.
- Be more interested in character than reputation.
- Know that valid self-analysis is crucial for improvement.

I encourage you to pick up Wooden's book and read it in full—there's much to learn from him about the core values that one should posses in order to fulfill the greatness one is capable of. And his wisdom and legacy continue to give us so much today, reminding us that without values and character, we can never truly win.

CHARACTER IN THE FACE OF ADVERSITY

When everything in your life is going smoothly, it's easy to possess and maintain a strong sense of character. True character is not unveiled or pushed to its greatest potential under these calm circumstances. True character remains dormant in our innermost selves until we come face-to-face with adversity. We can refer to the traditional maxim: when life gives you lemons, make lemonade. Sometimes this is easier said than done. It might be more likely that you will take a sour bite before taking the initiative to make lemonade.

Those who choose to take the bite are quick to react and fail to review the values that seemed so clear during times of good fortune. We all have the power to choose to make lemonade; it just takes some of us a little more time and a little more soul searching. You must determine your values and envision the person you would like to be when things stop going your way. You can either find yourself in a deeper rut than you were before or you can come out unscathed, but ultimately the choice is yours. If you are determined to come out unscathed when it's all said and done, then you are on your way to making lemonade. You can follow your values and build a stronger character that will help you deal with the curveballs that life throws your way. Character is not set in stone, but rather a foundation of the entire house that is your life. It's up to you to build your character to withstand the elements.

RUGBY WORLD CUP, 1995: SPIRITUAL CLARITY

The moment marked a significant shift—not only in sports but in world history as well. The 1995 South African Men's Rugby Team, the Springboks, were about to meet their match in the World Cup Final. Under coach Kitch Christie, the Springboks were undefeated. But so was their opponent, the New Zealand All Blacks.

The match intensified with each passing minute. The Springboks took the lead early on, with the All Blacks a safe distance behind at 9–6. But they didn't stay comfortable for long; the All Blacks made a comeback early in the second half, tying 9–9. As the game went into overtime, the Springboks saw their chance at the World Cup slipping through their fingers. With the score tied, one more successful play by the All Blacks would end the Springboks' undefeated winning streak and leave the South Africans sorely disappointed.

The two teams fought long and hard for the win, but one drop goal ended it. It was Springbok fly-half Joel Stransky to the rescue. His now-famous drop goal brought his team to a historic victory, as he kicked the ball right over the crossbar and won the match.

Yet not all the excitement of the 1995 World Cup resulted from the Springboks' victory. It was also a moment of victory over South Africa's very dark, very recent past. The recent end of apartheid meant an end to segregation between black and white South Africans that had kept whites in power. It began a time of great hope—and great uncertainty—for the nation, a step back toward character and ethics. With Nelson Mandela as president, South Africa began its healing process and its journey toward a brighter future.

That future never looked more promising than at that moment on June 24, 1995, as the Springboks celebrated their victory. The sun shone that bright day at Ellis Park in Johannesburg, and the buzzing excitement of South Africa's win filled the stadium. In the middle of it all stood François Pienaar, the Springboks' brawny, blond captain. It was an incredible day for Pienaar and his team; they were still undefeated, and they were about to be awarded the Rugby World Cup. What Pienaar didn't know was that winning the World Cup would be the least of his accomplishments that day.

President Nelson Mandela strode onto the field, clad in Pienaar's #6 jersey. He was carrying the World Cup trophy. Noticing, the crowd began to cheer and chant his name. *"Nelson! Nelson! Nelson!"*

Mandela approached Pienaar—two leaders brought together that day in celebration of sport: one young, white rubgy captain next to the older, black president. They could not have been any more different. But at that moment, something stronger than age, race, and history connected them forever: the victorious spirit. The two jovially shook hands, and Pienaar triumphantly hoisted the World Cup trophy over his head with Mandela smiling beside him. It was a dual celebration of physical achievement and the triumph of character. South Africa had won more than a rugby championship that day, and the cheering crowds were celebrating more than just a win for their athletes.

WHEN CHARACTER BREAKS DOWN

Temptation has a presence in everybody's life at some point or another. Sometimes the wrong choice seems so easy, yet still seems to go against every moral fiber in our bodies. Situations ranging from the everyday to the extraordinary provide a true test of the values that we live by and how we apply them. Like the old adage says: When a tree falls in the woods and no one is around to hear it, does it still make a sound? Well, sometimes when you go against your own values, you might think that nobody will find out. So did you actually break them? Character is more than doing a good deed simply because you know that the spotlight is on you. Character is adhering to your values in any given situation because you know that you couldn't sleep at night if you didn't abide by them. When it comes to character, there should be no gray areas—only the black or the white that screams out right or wrong. If you come across something that seems gray, it is usually wrong!

Being a public icon not only means that you must perform on the field but off of it as well. Athletes and coaches alike are held to a higher standard than those watching or reporting them. These public figures must both possess and demonstrate strong values to adhere by, or else their careers will take a sudden turn for the worse. For some, the desire to be the best can cloud their brains like a drug. They become intoxicated by the fame. They live in the here and now but fail to take into account the legacy that they will one day leave behind.

LANCE ARMSTRONG

Lance Armstrong, long considered an American hero, was once one of the most celebrated athletes in the world. His story was one of the great romances—he triumphed through a devastating medical tribulation only to come out even more successful than he was before. Armstrong's values of discipline, skill, and endurance were once something to be admired but, unfortunately, as his deceitfulness has now been exposed, we can see how much character really counts.

In June of 2012, the United States Anti-Doping Agency charged Armstrong with having used illegal performance-enhancing drugs during his time as a competitive cyclist. First, he vehemently denied these allegations. Armstrong was stripped of his seven Tour de France titles and his dignity. He stepped down from Livestrong, a nonprofit organization that he founded and that provides support to people living with cancer, and was barred from all Olympic competition. Yet he still denied the charges.

But just a few months later, in January of 2013, he changed his tune. In a surprisingly unemotional and unenergetic interview with Oprah Winfrey, he confessed to the doping. Yet he seemed to rationalize his decision to take the drugs as "necessary" and "to even the playing field." While he can be commended for finally coming clean, he did so in the same tone that he used as he dispassionately lied about it in the first place.

The serious doping allegations against Armstrong and his subsequent lack of sincerity have tarnished the image of this American athlete. The use of performance-enhancing drugs goes against all the core values that are characteristic of the victorious spirit. Armstrong's legacy and reputation have become irreparably damaged. His fall from grace was a fast and steep one. Lance Armstrong is living proof of how much character really does count.

BASEBALL'S "STEROID AGE"

Barry Bonds and Mark McGwire are two of the most famous names in baseball history. About ten years ago, these all-star athletes competed with each other for the prestigious title of home-run champion. Fans whooped and cheered when Bonds surpassed McGwire's record by batting his seventy-third home run in a single season. These elite athletes were modern marvels, breaking records left and right with incredible strength training and discipline.

Wrong. Years after the fame and fortune washed over these record breakers, the *San Francisco Chronicle* broke the devastating news to the world, as well as the MLB, that these men had been abusing steroids during their careers, thus their records were undeserved. Bonds tried to fight the allegations, protesting that he never knowingly took any illegal substances.

McGwire owned up to his steroid use in a tearful public admittance in 2010. He did not lie or make excuses and he publicly repented in the wake of the scandal, but that was not enough to restore his public image.

Both players were swept away in the high stakes competition for home-run records, and neither was able to distance himself from the temptation of the easy road to success. People have called for a change to be noted in baseball's history, excluding both players and stripping their records. Both Bonds and McGwire lacked the character to be truly victorious, and their legacies will be overshadowed by their devastating descent into disgrace rather than by their true talent.

• • •

Much like snowflakes, no two people are exactly alike. We all have different traits and features that make us unique. Character is not something that you inherit, like your hair or eye color; character is constantly being built upon by the decisions that we make on a daily basis. Robert Frost once said, "Two roads diverge in a yellow wood, and sorry I could not travel both."[37] When adversity or temptation arises, we are met with more than one path. Which path we take depends on our character. Just because one path appears to be paved with gold does not mean that it does not eventually turn to dirt. Those who choose the golden path cut corners and fail to adhere to values that are crucial to the character-building process. The glamour of instant gratification overshadows the reality of how it can affect our future. When it all falls apart, a lack of experience in dealing with adversity can leave us in a much worse situation than before. Nothing in life is free, and with every new path we must start from dirt and build our own golden road. The adversities we face along the way are all important building blocks to help us define the kind of person we want to become. The victorious spirit is not something we can achieve through cheating. In order to fully grasp it, we must persevere through turmoil and stick to a set of strong values that help us weather the storm.

PART III

APPLYING
THE BIG FIVE

CHAPTER 9

Mission, Vision, Plan

The Path to Being Your Own MVP

It's a funny thing about life; if you refuse to
accept anything but the best, you very often get it.
—W. Somerset Maugham

I COULD GO ON AND ON about the nature of the victorious spirit—
how it's hardwired within us, how it drives us through adversity, how
it brings us together as one. And I could write all day about any one of
the Big Five: the importance of eating right and exercising, the power
of optimism and hope, the transformative capacity of rich experiences,
the value of relationships and kindness, and the weight of character. I
could tell many more stories about teamwork and the abounding compassion in the world. I could relay countless stories of epic Olympic
triumphs and the modern gladiators who react to a snapped femur like
it's a sprained pinky. I could offer more evidence of the innate victorious
spirit and athlete in all of us.

But, that would just be more words in a book. As words, these concepts are only concepts, niceties at best and clichés at worst. There's a

danger that, left on the page, they become hollow to us, walkless talks and biteless barks. That's why I want to end this book on a practical note.

There's only one way to actualize the Big Five and imbed these principles in your life. How? Through action! Through living out these concepts. You have the choice of reading the words on this page, putting the book down, and continuing your life along the same lines as you were before you picked up this book. Or, you can make the decision to change your habits, integrate some new paradigms into your thinking, and start looking at the world differently. If your attitude changes, your behavior is likely to follow suit pretty quickly. Making the decision to eat your vegetables or run to the post office rather than drive is not a major inconvenience in your life. Yet, shifting your approach to food or how you move your body can be the first step in a life change that will have major repercussions on how you look, how you feel, and how you perform. Even if you don't do it for the right reasons, do it because you will simply *feel* so much better. Recognizing the impact on your sense of well-being when you begin to access the victorious spirit within you is a gift that you cannot fully appreciate until you try.

We all, for example, understand what optimism means; we all know what a relationship is. But the secret to finding contentment and fulfillment in your life is not understanding optimism, but living optimistically. It is not about intellectualizing the value of relationships, but diving in and allowing yourself to connect at an emotional level with someone else. Go ahead and *care* about your buddies at work or the barista who makes your coffee every day. These aren't transactions—these are the jewels of life. Allow yourself to be vulnerable and take the risk of full engagement.

Olympic heroes are apt role models because they not only possess the proper mentalities, but they also employ them in each of their choices and actions. Tim Daggett wasn't just reluctant to quit; he trained relentlessly to get back in the Olympics. Ernest Shackleton wasn't just optimistic; he trekked, sailed, and navigated through ice for two years. Jesse Billauer isn't just compassionate; he brings smiles to one hundred thousand spinal cord injured victims a year. No one can act meaningfully without the proper mindset, but, without real-world choices and thoughtful actions, a mentality is worthless. Our lives are measured not by what we think, but what we do. Our world isn't judged by what it could be, but what it is.

I don't want to make it seem like I think finding success is as easy as getting off the couch and walking out the door. It's not. Let's face it: we don't live in a Cinderella world where serendipity serves us a life of fortune on a silver platter. This too is a journey of discovery, incorporation, and integration and it may be a major paradigm change. It's easy to read about any one of the Big Five and spend the next few hours focused on living them out. That's wonderful, and there's benefit to every positive action you take to enhance your victorious spirit. Very rarely, however, does a single action turn an entire life around. We have to be practical and accept that the path to individual success and happiness is an incremental and systematic progression. We must find a way to integrate the Big Five—and the actions that support them—into our lives for the long term.

In order to start down that path, we need a strategy. I call it the "MVP process"—you set a Mission, flesh it out into a Vision, and then set your Plan. Mission, Vision, Plan: it's your guide to becoming your own MVP.

MISSION

Discovering your mission is where the path to success begins, and where the conceptual plays its strongest role in strategizing success. We all have passions and life goals—professional, personal, or social—that we value more highly than our other simple desires. We all need a motivating purpose in life, and so we need to make it our mission to fulfill those aspects of ourselves that we feel are truly essential to our character.

At this early stage, we must find personal strength and courage to face our goals head-on. This is where our evolutionary athleticism comes into play, as we need to harness our innate thirst for betterment, mustering the energy that we will need further down the road. A mission is a commitment, and so we need to develop a faith in our goals and a trust in ourselves in order to dedicate our entire being to the completion of them. Once we declare our mission, we have to continue to distinguish it from a simple wish or want so that when we hit those inevitable roadblocks along the way, we will be too invested to quit.

Celestine Chua, Personal Excellence Coach and founder of Personal Excellence, differentiates between two concepts of "purpose"— imposed purposes and liberating purposes.[38] Imposed purposes are those that you do not take on willingly—they are "imposed" on you by your friends, your family, or your coworkers. They are what you think others want you to do, or what others need you to do. They are driven by fear—of letting someone else down. In this way, you may come to dread them. While the fulfillment of these purposes may cause temporary satisfaction, in the end you are unfulfilled because imposed purposes are not *your* purposes. Your purposes are liberating. They are your personal choice, and completely inspired by you. They resonate with you and they are driven by love, hope, and passion. They are empowering and energizing, and the fulfillment of them leaves you happy and full of meaning.

What are your imposed purposes? What do you do simply because others ask of you, whether implicitly or explicitly? Ditch these hollow purposes. They will only leave you uninspired. Ask yourself what you want to do for you, what you love, what you are passionate about, and what you lose time over because you lose yourself in it.

In the mission-setting stage, we begin to treat our dreams not as dreams, but as realities that are simply yet to happen. We begin to put the pieces in place, establishing a foundational groundwork from where we will ascend. (Later, in the planning stage, we'll form relationships; we'll adventure; we'll do all the things that will eventually contribute to the completion of the mission.)

As you iron out your mission, ask yourself the following questions:

- How do I measure success?
- What makes me happy?

- What are the barriers to my success? What will stop me from just doing it?

By defining these concepts, you'll be more prepared to see the bigger picture and to set realistic goals for yourself.

In her article "Life on Purpose," Tina Su developed fifteen questions to ask yourself in order to find your personal mission. [39] The most salient ones asked:

- What makes you smile?
- What do people typically ask you for help in?
- If you could get a message across to a large group of people, who would they be and what would be your message?
- What would you regret doing, or not doing, by the end of your life?

Answer these questions. Are you seeing a general theme? You are beginning to define your purpose, and thereby your mission.

In developing your mission, you also need to think about your core values. Core values are the elements that make you who you are, that sit at the core of your being. They might include any of the following: accomplishment, authority, recognition, leadership, security, money, advancement, service, religion, health, integrity, country, excitement, philanthropy, and family. Make your own list of all the values that are important to you, then read it over to see which two or three are more important than the others. Keep refining until you have a short list that's truly unique to you. These are your core values.

All this work comes down to the development of your mission statement. The mission statement confirms and expresses your purpose. It's a commitment that carries you toward your goals and objectives. It is your personal constitution. The mission focuses on who you want to be in terms of character and what you want as it relates to contribution and accomplishment. It starts with seeing the world around you: looking in the mirror, seeing the person staring back at you, defining what the problem is, and assessing it.

Now take a stab at writing the mission statement. A great place to start is by figuring out the main problem you're facing. Write it down in one single sentence saying, "The problem is:_____." It might be that you have gained forty pounds and the doctor has said that you are in the beginning stage of diabetes. Make it your first priority to define, know, and understand this problem.

Now, write the mission statement, but expressing how you want to live, given that problem. What direction do you want to be headed in? Take your time, and be clear and concise, focused and purposeful. Here are some examples:

- My mission is to take care of my family and my health and to be the best oboist I can be in the orchestra.
- My mission is to be a psychologist and give back to my community in every possible way that I can.
- My mission is to raise my children to be kind and happy and be the best that they are capable of becoming.

It may take days or weeks to refine your exact mission. It will need to stand the test of time, and it should never be wholly changed, just amended. The mission is the foundation of the ultimate executed plan. It is nonnegotiable. It is truly reflective of who and what you are!

VISION

With your mission in place, we move on to the "V" of the MVP process: Vision. This is where we fully flesh out the details of where our mission is taking us. Our vision takes on a more realistic and practical hue than the bold proclamation of a life mission, but this is still a mental exercise. We're still allowing ourselves to dream big. (For as Eleanor Roosevelt said, "The future belongs to those who believe in the beauty of their dreams.")[40]

As we fill in the full vision, we become ideal realists in imagining our success, anticipating the technical aspects of the path, but doing so without compromising our idealistic motivation. Dream of your ideal situation, but in a realistic framework. Don't set yourself up for disappointment with grand, unattainable fantasies, but don't sell yourself short, either. Realism is not synonymous with cynicism. Find the reasonable medium of optimism, between misleading impracticality and inhibitive doubt.

Your vision statement is an inspirational personal statement that states where you want to be in the future while guiding and communicating both your purpose and values. It starts with your dreams and connects to how and where they will take you in the future. Developing your vision statement isn't something that should be rushed, so sit quietly and reflect on some basic issues:

- What are the most important values for me and how do I actualize and implement them in the next one, two, and five years?
- How do I get there?
- What are my strengths, weaknesses, and opportunities?
- Where are the obstacles?

This statement should be bold and idealistic but should also have some realistic flavors to it. It's a little longer than the mission statement, and it can also be tied to one or more of the Big Five—exercise and nutrition, optimism and hope, adventure and challenges, relationships and mentoring, or values and character. Base your vision statement around whichever you see as being the most fundamental to taking you to the place described in your mission statement.

Let's look at some sample vision statements so you can practice:

- I want to be a leader among men and help all the people who I meet. I want to be an inspirational leader and educator globally.

I'd love to be a truthful, family person and want to travel across the world and enjoy life with rich experiences.

- My life vision is to serve children through teaching art that enriches children's lives. I will do this with a team of individuals determined to work together in excellence and to truly see our dreams come true.

Using these examples as a starting point, sit down and think about your own vision. What do you see for yourself in the future?

Now that you've developed your mission and vision, you need a game plan.

PLAN

In sports and in life, you need a strategy, a game plan. In order to create a successful game plan—the "P" of MVP—you must prepare for and anticipate the range of the possibilities that await you. Look at the challenges, the meetings, the ways that you manage, and the jobs that you apply for from every angle. Anticipate the good and the bad, and think of questions or possible problems that could arise. Doing so gives you an edge and puts you on top when others might fall.

There is an old military adage known as the "Eight Ps": "Proper prior planning and preparation prevents piss poor performance." The expression is used to stress the importance that preparation has on your overall performance. Like a soldier's preparation for battle, we must all go through the rigorous preparation process in order to prevent a "piss poor performance." Being the best might feel like it comes naturally to some, but that is not the case. It must be earned though the preparation and practice that your coaches, teachers, and parents put you through. If you plan strategically and practice harder than your opponent, whether it is a rival team or an opposing individual, you will be the one celebrating in the end. The same can be said in all walks of life. In academics, your final grade is not a reflection of how smart you are, but rather how motivated you were and how much planning and effort you put in before the final. As the old saying goes, "If you fail to plan, you plan to fail."

When we were young, our parents didn't just throw us in a swimming pool hoping that we would innately know how to swim. They prepared us, they helped us, they kept our tiny heads afloat, and they showed us how to wiggle our tiny arms. Your dreams and goals are just as important. Any type of preparation involves an idea that precedes the action, a blueprint of how to get the job done effectively—a plan. Like houses, our plans would surely crumble without some form of guidance to lead us.

By now you should already have an idea of your core values, strengths, and vision, so developing them into a strategy should not be as intimidating. Though sometimes it can feel awkward and difficult to self-examine and then write about it. But as Nike says, just do it!

Remember when you are answering these questions that no goal is too lofty. There is no such thing as being too ambitious! It's true that winners and successful people make mistakes. But mistakes are how you learn and how you mold and create the goals you truly want to achieve in your life. If you're not making mistakes, then you are not succeeding. This too is a journey of discovery, incorporation, and integration and it may be a major paradigm change. Remember that bad experiences help make good judgments and unimagined opportunities.

• • •

In the days and weeks ahead, spend your time introspectively. This will help you to develop the process of what and who you are and who you want to be. You are the pilot, and you should have comfort in this process. Make it your priority to know your strengths, weaknesses, and opportunities! Discover, identify, and focus on your strengths by fine-tuning your confidence. In every successful person, there are some common threads, but each individual has a very different combination of attributes, values, and skills. Some of us are big-picture visionaries while others are fine-tuned operational machines. Some of us are also a scalable blend of the extremes of vision or operation.

What do all of these things mean? They represent your path to success, achievements, and your overall happiness. Unfortunately, this isn't some futuristic book that can change your life simply by you reading it. There is another part to making this book work to your advantage—that part is you. The hope is that it will motivate YOU to continue on, past this book to a life worth living. It's now up to you to take what you've learned and apply it to your life. As we know, we live the life that we want. It's up to you to make a change for the better. Nothing is too far away, too far-fetched, or too unachievable. You have to take the steps to get where you want to be no matter how small, and you have to start right now! The great thing about life is that it is a great and all-encompassing journey with many chances and unimagined opportunities. You are ready for a change in your life, even if it is a refinement. It is always worthwhile to evaluate, discover, and integrate a new interpretation, perception, or a new approach. The only constant is change and real strength comes from the adaptive progressions in response. Remember, you are one of the survivors of the fittest. You have been programmed that way. It is in you. Find it, embrace it, and nourish it; focus, plan, and create. You are destined to not only survive but to thrive. So go do it! Be the master of your destiny, the captain of your fate.

With these three stages of strategizing success laid out, you become the MVP of your own life. With a mission, you can envision, and with a vision, you can plan. Once you have your plan fully fleshed out, the rest should be gravy. You'll have the inner passion to persist, the mental stability to merge hope with practicality, and the context to properly frame and guide you to being victorious and finding your win within. It is this flame that burns within you that honors past sacrifices, highlights present successes, and illuminates the path to future glories.

This awareness and readiness—in conjunction with your set of tools, the Big Five—enhances the probability that you will find expression for the victorious spirit within you.

Epilogue

WE ARE ALL SURVIVORS. WE ARE all dreamers. We are all victors. We evolved from the same human ancestors, back when there were no sports or competitions besides the challenge of survival. We learned to hunt, to gather, to think, to develop, and to adapt. While we are all unique with our own strengths, weaknesses, passions, and motivations, we are all similar too. We all experience joy, as I was reminded as the American celebrating among the Iraqis. We all experience embarrassment, as unhappily revealed to us by Lance Armstrong's fall from grace. But what we all have that truly brings us together as humans is the victorious spirit that resides inside each and every one of us.

You may not realize yet that you have it. Take it from me, I did not understand my victorious spirit for years. I went through life with ups and downs, not appreciating adversity as the engine of unimagined opportunities. First, I was cut from the football team in high school. I thought I had failed my passion and would never be an athlete. Then I was rejected from medical school, another opportunity that I could've sworn was meant to be. There were times that I saw myself as a failure, rejected by every medical school to which I applied. But, luckily, I was surrounded by mentors and a team who helped me reclaim my idea of "self." I responded with a dedication to a new mission, vision, and plan. I found my victorious spirit and my win within. And when I tried again to get into medical school, I was admitted to every school to which I applied. I was right all along—I could do it. But this time, I was prepared and ready for it. I had discovered my victorious spirit in the process.

Right time, right place, right person. Perhaps the most important thing in life is to be your own "right" person. Take the tools that I have given you and assess who you are. What drives you? What makes you happy? Don't be inhibited by your own misgivings. Dare to dream like Tim Daggett when he proved that he could get back into Olympic-shape after snapping his leg in two. Live and think as a "we," thinking about living dynamically with compassion and kindness with all of your interactions. I hope to be a mentor to you, a Bill Belichick to your Tom Brady. Together, we can be a TEAM: Together Everyone Achieves More.

Remember Charlie Davies, Ernest Shackleton, and the ragtag group who turned out to be a miracle hockey team. Be a fighter, be a survivor, and be a team member. When faced with a challenge, remember to always engage in fair play and respect and to not take the easy way out. Don't be Lance Armstrong, not facing up to his accusers; don't be Barry Bonds, cheating in order to quickly succeed. Appreciate with perspective your successes and defeats. Never too high, and never letting yourself go too low. Success takes hard work, determination, perseverance, and an unwillingness to give up. Refuse to be anything but the best you are capable of becoming. The victorious spirit that you will find inside will make all the difference.

Be rich in your experiences. Be happy in your choices. Be fulfilled in your life. Dig deep to create your mission, vision, and plan. You are now ready to be your own MVP: Most Valuable Player. You are ready to be victorious and discover that the win is right there—within!

Notes

CHAPTER 1: HARDWIRED FOR VICTORY

1. I am indebted to the following publications for much of the information contained in this section: A. G. Morris, "Isolation and the Origin of the Khoisan: Late Pleistocene and Early Holocene Human Evolution at the Southern End of Africa," *Human Evolution* 17, no. 3–4 (July–December, 2002): 231–240; C. Sandholzer et al., "High Frequency of the Apo Epsilon 4 Allele in Khoi San from South Africa," *Human Genetics* 95, no. 1 (January, 1995): 46–48; Laurent Excoffier et al., "Genetics and History of Sub-Saharan Africa," *Supplement: American Journal of Physical Anthropology* 30, no. S8 (1987): 151–194.

2. Dennis M. Bramble and Daniel E. Lieberman, "Endurance Running and the Evolution of *Homo*," *Nature* 432 (November 18, 2004): 345–352.

3. Daniel Lieberman and Dennis Bramble, "The Evolution of Marathon Running," *Sports Medicine* 37, no. 4–5: 288–290.

4. David Raichlen et al., "Wired to Run," *Journal of Experimental Biology* 215 (April 15, 2012): 1331–1336.

5. David Epstein, "Sports Genes," *Sports Illustrated* 112, no. 21 (May 17, 2010): 53–65.

CHAPTER 2: MEND IT LIKE BECKHAM

6. John Reger, *Quotable Wooden* (Lanham, MD: Taylor Trade Publishing, 2012).

CHAPTER 3: THE COLLECTIVE VICTORIOUS SPIRIT

7. I am indebted to the following publication for much of the information contained in this section: Robert Garland, *Daily Life of the Ancient Greeks* (Westport, CT: Greenwood, 2008).

8. Allan Massie, "London Olympics 2012: The Olympic Values of Fair Play and Sportsmanship Are Stamped 'Made in Britain,'" *Telegraph*, July 30, 2012.

9. Paul Begaud, Vanessa Corish, and Wayne Tester, "Dare to Dream."

10. "Winnipegger Heads to NY for 9-11 Memorial," CBC News, September 9, 2011.

CHAPTER 4: LIFE'S ELIXIRS

11. Kathleen Doheny, "Post-Exercise 'Glow' May Last 12 Hours," *HealthDay*, May 29, 2009.

12. *World Alzheimer Report 2011*, Alzheimer's Disease International, 2011, http://www.alz.co.uk/research/world-report-2011.

13. "Ray Allen's Guide to Being a Celtic," YouTube video, https://www.youtube.com/watch?v=OR24EYSPL1A.

14. Shannon Alllen, "Ray Allen's Diet and Workout," CelebrityDietDoctor.com, July 5, 2010.

15. Kelley Carter, "Shannon Allen, Ray's Wife, Talks About Cooking," ESPN.com, January 17, 2012.

16. Joanne Eglash, "Slideshow: Dara Torres Reveals Diet Secrets for Competing in Olympics at Age 45," Examiner.com, July 2, 2012.

17. Karina Arrue, "Dara Torres on Her Diet, How She Plans on Staying in Shape, and Life After Swimming," Glamour.com, September 9, 2009.

18. "Letters About Nolan Ryan," http://www.nolanryan.net/nolanryan.net/A_Hero_To_Us_All.html.

CHAPTER 5: THE RAMPARTS OF VICTORY: OPTIMISM AND HOPE

19. I am indebted to the following publications for much of the information contained in this section: Alfred Lansing, *Endurance: Shackleton's Incredible Voyage* (New York City: Basic Books, 1999); Elizabeth Cody Kimmel, *Ice Story: Shackleton's Lost Expedition* (New York City: Clarion Books, 1999).

20. Lisa Ocker, "A Wonderful Life," *Success*, June 28, 2009, http://www.success.com/article/a-wonderful-life.

21. Michael J. Fox, *Always Looking Up* (New York: Hyperion, 2009).

22. Ibid.

23. Lee Jenkins, "With a New Spirit, the Red Sox Tackle Their Haunted Past," *New York Times*, October 12, 2004.

24. Bob Ryan, "Even by Their Standards, This Is a New Low," *Boston Globe*, October 17, 2004.

CHAPTER 6: CREATING RICH EXPERIENCES: ADVENTURE AND CHALLENGES

25. Jonah Fisher, "Pregnant Malaysian Shooter Eyes Olympic Gold," BBC News Asia, July 24, 2012.

26. Ibid.

27. Adam Shergold, "Shooting for Two!" *Daily Mail*, July 26, 2012.

28. Chris Chase, "Pregnant Shooter Will Compete in London Olympics," *Yahoo! Sports*, April 13, 2012.

CHAPTER 7: THE JEWELS OF LIFE: RELATIONSHIPS AND MENTORING

29. Jan Stradling, *More Than a Game* (St. Leonards, NSW: Pier 9, 2009).

30. Kevin Allen, *USA Hockey* (Chicago, IL: Triumph Books, 1997).

31. Scott T. Allison and George R. Goethals, *Heroic Leadership: A Taxonomy of 100 Exceptional Individuals* (New York: Routledge, 2013).

32. I am indebted to the following publication for much of the information contained in this section: Angelo Dundee, *My View From the Corner: A Life in Boxing* (New York: McGraw Hill, 2008).

33. Angelo Dundee, *My View From the Corner: A Life in Boxing* (New York: McGraw Hill, 2008).

34. Michael Benson, *Winning Words: Classic Quotes From the World of Sports* (Lanham, MD: Taylor Trade Publishing, 2008).

CHAPTER 8: FAIR PLAY

35. "The Six Pillars of Character," *CharacterCounts.org*, Josephson Institute, 2012.

36. Reger, *Quotable Wooden*.

CHAPTER 9: MISSION, VISSION, PLAN

37. Robert Frost, "The Road Not Taken," *Mountain Interval* (New York City: Henry Holt and Company, 1916).

38. Celestine Chua, "Why Earning Money Is Not Your Real Purpose (And How to Know What Is)," PersonalExcellence.com.

39. Ibid.

40. Leonard C. Schlup and Donald W. Whisenhunt, *It Seems to Me: Selected Letters of Eleanor Roosevelt* (Lexington, KY: University Press of Kentucky, 2001): 2.

Selected Bibliography

Allison, Scott T. and George R. Goethals. *Heroic Leadership: A Taxonomy of 100 Exceptional Individuals*. New York: Routledge, 2013.

Benson, Michael. *Winning Words: Classic Quotes from the World of Sports*. Lanham, MD: Taylor Trade Publishing, 2008.

Bramble, Dennis M. and Daniel E. Lieberman. "Endurance Running and the Evolution of Homo." *Nature* 432 (November 18, 2004): 345–352.

Cody Kimmel, Elizabeth. *Ice Story: Shackleton's Lost Expedition*. New York City: Clarion Books, 1999.

Dundee, Angelo. *My View From the Corner: A Life in Boxing*. New York: McGraw Hill, 2008.

Epstein, David. "Sports Genes." *Sports Illustrated* 112, no. 21 (May 17, 2010): 53–65.

Excoffier, Laurent et al. "Genetics and History of Sub-Saharan Africa." *Supplement: American Journal of Physical Anthropology* 30, no. S8 (1987): 151–194.

Fox, Michael J. *Always Looking Up*. New York: Hyperion, 2009.

Garland, Robert. *Daily Life of the Ancient Greeks*. Westport, CT: Greenwood, 2008.

Lansing, Alfred. *Endurance: Shackleton's Incredible Voyage*. New York City: Basic Books, 1999.

Lieberman, Daniel and Dennis Bramble. "The Evolution of Marathon Running." *Sports Medicine* 37 (4–5): 288–290.

Morris, A. G. "Isolation and the Origin of the Khoisan: Late Pleistocene and Early Holocene Human Evolution at the Southern End of Africa." *Human Evolution* 17, no. 3–4 (July–December, 2002): 231–240.

Raichlen, David et al. "Wired to Run." *Journal of Experimental Biology* 215 (April 15, 2012): 1331–1336.

Reger, John. *Quotable Wooden*. Lanham, MD: Taylor Trade Publishing, 2012.

Sandholzer, C. et al. "High Frequency of the Apo Epsilon 4 Allele in Khoi San from South Africa." *Human Genetics* 95, no. 1 (January 1995): 46–48.

Stradling, Jan. *More Than a Game*. St. Leonards, NSW: Pier 9, 2009.

Index

About the Author

BERT MANDELBAUM RECEIVED HIS MEDICAL DEGREE in 1980 from Washington University Medical School in St. Louis, MO. He went on to complete his residency in Orthopaedic Surgery at The Johns Hopkins Hospital and a fellowship in Sports Medicine at UCLA, where he also served as a faculty member from 1986–1989 before going into private medical practice.

Dr. Mandelbaum currently is among the world's foremost experts in the prevention, diagnosis, and treatment of orthopedic conditions, especially those related to the knee. He spends most of his time at his clinical practice, Santa Monica Orthopaedic and Sports Medicine Group, helping heal patients who have experienced orthopedic injury, as well as serving as the practice's director of both the Sports Medicine Fellowship Program and the Research and Education Foundation. He is also the co-chair of medical affairs for the Institute for Sports Sciences in Los Angeles.

Due to his vast expertise, Dr. Mandelbaum is sought after by some of the world's most prestigious athletes and athletic organizations. He has served as team physician for numerous collegiate and MLS teams, as well as the US Soccer Men's National Team. He currently serves as the medical director for the FIFA Medical Center of Excellence in Santa Monica, the director of research for Major League Baseball, and also serves on the USOC National Medical Network Advisory Group. Most recently, Dr. Mandelbaum was appointed as chief medical officer for the 2015 World Special Olympic Games.

Married for more than twenty years to his wife Ruth, a family physician, the couple has three children: Rachel, Jordan, and Ava. Since life is absolutely a TEAM sport, Dr. Mandelbaum considers his accomplishments in life a direct result of his strong, supportive, and comforting family.